Victory Over Vice

Also by Fulton J. Sheen
from Sophia Institute Press®:

God's World and Our Place in It

Fulton J. Sheen

Victory Over Vice

SOPHIA INSTITUTE PRESS®
Manchester, New Hampshire

Victory Over Vice was originally published in 1939 by
Garden City Books, Garden City, New York. This 2004 edition by
Sophia Institute Press contains minor editorial revisions.
Copyright © 2004 Sophia Institute Press

Printed in the United States of America.

Sophia Institute Press
Box 5284, Manchester, NH 03108
1-800-888-9344
www.SophiaInstitute.com
Sophia Institute Press® is a registered trademark of Sophia Institute.

Cover image courtesy of The Archbishop Fulton J. Sheen Foundation.

Nihil Obstat: Arthur J. Scanlan, S.T.D.. *Censor Librorum.*
Imprimatur: Stephen J. Donahue, D.D., Adm., New York,
New York, April 1, 1939.

Library of Congress Cataloging-in-Publication Data

Sheen, Fulton J. (Fulton John), 1895-1979.
Victory over vice / Fulton J. Sheen.
    p. cm.
  ISBN 1-928832-30-X (pbk. : alk. paper)
1. Jesus Christ — Seven last words — Meditations.
2. Deadly sins — Meditations. I. Title.
  BT457 .S54 2004
232.96'35 — dc22

                          2003024655

Dedicated to
the Mother of Sorrows
in humble petition
for victory over vice

⚹

Contents

Editor's note: The biblical quotations in the following pages are taken from the Douay-Rheims edition of the Old and New Testaments. Where applicable, quotations have been cross-referenced with the differing names and enumeration in the Revised Standard Version, using the following symbol: (RSV =).

❦

Victory Over Vice

First Word

※

Anger

"Father, forgive them, for
they know not what they do."

Luke 23:34

The one passion in man that has deeper roots in his rational nature than any other is the passion of anger. Anger and reason are capable of great compatibility, because anger is based upon reason, which weighs the injury done and the satisfaction to be demanded. We are never angry unless someone has injured us in some way — or we think he has.

But not all anger is sinful, for there is such a thing as just anger. The most perfect expression of just anger we find in our blessed Lord's cleansing the Temple. Passing through its shadowed doorways at the festival of the Pasch, He found greedy traders, victimizing at every turn the worshipers who needed lambs and doves for the Temple sacrifices.

Making a scourge of little cords, He moved through their midst with a calm dignity and beautiful self-control even more compelling than the whip. The oxen and sheep He drove out with His scourge. With His hands, He upset the tables of the money-changers, who scrambled on the floor after their rolling coins. With His finger, He pointed to the vendors of doves and bade them leave the outer court. To all He said, "Take these things hence, and make not the house of my Father a house of traffic."[1]

Here was fulfilled the injunction of the Scriptures, "Be angry, and sin not,"[2] for anger is no sin under three conditions: if the cause of anger is just, for example, defense of God's honor; if it is no greater than the cause demands, that is, if it is kept under control; and if it is quickly subdued: "Let not the sun go down upon your anger."[3]

Here we are not concerned with just anger, but with unjust anger, namely, that which has no rightful cause — anger that is excessive, revengeful, and enduring; the kind

[1] John 2:16.
[2] Eph. 4:26.
[3] Ibid.

of anger and hatred against God that has destroyed religion on one-sixth of the earth's surface; the kind of hatred that is not only directed against God, but also against fellowmen, and is fanned by the disciples of class conflict who talk peace but glory in war; the red anger that rushes the blood to the surface, and the white anger that pushes it to the depths and bleaches the face; the anger that seeks to get even, to repay in kind, bump for bump, punch for punch, eye for eye, lie for lie; the anger of the clenched fist prepared to strike, not in defense of that which is loved, but in offense against that which is hated; in a word, the kind of anger that will destroy our civilization unless we smother it by love.

Our blessed Lord came to make reparation for the sin of anger, first by teaching us a prayer: "Forgive us our trespasses as we forgive those who trespass against us"; and then by giving us a precept: "Love your enemies; do good to them that hate you."[4] More concretely still, He added, "Whosoever will force thee one mile, go with him another two. . . . If a man . . . take away thy coat, let go thy cloak also unto him."[5]

---

[4] Matt. 5:44; Luke 6:27.
[5] Matt. 5:40, 41.

Revenge and retaliation were forbidden: "You have heard that it has been said: an eye for an eye, and a tooth for a tooth. But I say unto you, love your enemies."[6] These precepts were made all the more striking because our Lord practiced them.

When the Gerasenes became angry at Him because He put a higher value on an afflicted man than on a herd of swine, Scripture records no retort: "And entering into the boat, He passed over the water."[7] To the soldier who struck Him with a mailed fist, He meekly responded "If I have spoken evil, give testimony of the evil, but if well, why strikest thou me?"[8]

The perfect reparation for anger was made on Calvary. We might also say that anger and hate led our Lord up that hill. His own people hated Him, for they asked for His crucifixion; the law hated Him, for it forsook justice to condemn Justice; the Gentiles hated Him, for they consented to His death; the forests hated Him for one of its trees bore the burden of His weight; the flowers hated Him as they wove thorns for His brow; the bowels

---

[6] Matt. 5:38, 44.

[7] Matt. 9:1.

[8] John 18:23.

of the earth hated Him as it gave its steel as hammer and nails.

Then, as if to personalize all that hatred, the first generation of clenched fists in the history of the world stood beneath the Cross and shook them in the face of God. Even today, the hearts of their descendants freeze into fists.

As we contemplate those clenched fists, we cannot help but feel that if ever anger would have been justified, if ever Justice might have fittingly judged, if ever Power might have rightfully struck, if ever Innocence might have lawfully protested, if ever God might have justly revenged Himself against man — it was at that moment.

And yet, just at that second when a sickle and a hammer combined to cut down the grass on Calvary's hill to erect a cross, and drive nails through hands to render impotent the blessings of Love incarnate, He, like a tree that bathes in perfume the axe that kills it, lets fall from His lips for the earth's first hearing the perfect reparation for anger and hate: a prayer for the army of clenched fists, the first Word from the Cross: "Father, forgive them, for they know not what they do."

The greatest sinner may now be saved; the blackest sin may now be blotted out; the clenched fist may now be opened; the unforgivable may now be forgiven. While they were most certain that they knew what they were doing, He seizes upon the only possible palliation of their crime and urges it upon His heavenly Father with all the ardor of a merciful Heart: ignorance — "They know not what they do." If they *did* know what they were doing as they fastened Love to a tree, and still went on doing it, they would never be saved. They would be damned.

It is only because fists are clenched in ignorance that they may yet be opened into folded hands; it is only because tongues blaspheme in ignorance that they may yet speak in prayer. It is not their conscious wisdom that saves them; it is their unconscious ignorance.

This Word from the Cross teaches us two lessons: the reason for forgiving is ignorance; and there are no limits to forgiveness.

The reason for forgiving is ignorance. Divine Innocence found such a reason for pardon; certainly guilt can do no less. St. Peter's first Pentecost sermon used this very excuse of ignorance for the Crucifixion so fresh in his mind: "The author of life you killed . . . and now, brethren, I know that you did it through ignorance, as did also your rulers."[9]

---

[9] Acts 3:15, 17.

If there were full consciousness of the evil, perfect deliberation, perfect understanding of the consequences of acts, there would be no room for forgiveness. That is why there is no redemption for the fallen angels. They knew what they were doing. We do not. We are very ignorant — ignorant of ourselves and ignorant of others.

Ignorant of others! How little we know of their motives, their good faith, the circumstances surrounding their actions. When others visit violence upon us, we, too, often forget how little we know about their hearts and say, "I cannot see that they have the slightest excuse; they knew very well what they were doing." And yet in exactly the same circumstances, Jesus found an excuse: "They know not what they do."

We know nothing about the inside of our neighbor's heart, and hence, we refuse to forgive. Jesus knew the heart inside out, and because He did know, He forgave. Take any scene of action, let five people look upon it, and you will get five different stories of what happened. No one of them sees all sides. Our Lord does, and that is why He forgives.

Why is it that we can find excuses for our anger against our neighbor, yet we refuse to admit the same excuses when our neighbor is angry with us? We say others would forgive us if they understood us perfectly, and that the only reason they are angry with us is because "they do not understand."

Why is not that ignorance reversible? Can we not be as ignorant of their motives, as we say they are ignorant of ours? Does not our refusal to find an excuse for their hatred tacitly mean that, under similar circumstances, we ourselves will be unfit to be forgiven?

Ignorance of ourselves is another reason for forgiving others. Unfortunately it is ourselves we know least; our neighbor's sins, weaknesses, and failures we know a thousand times better than our own. Criticism of others may be bad, but it is want of self-criticism which is worse.

It would be less wrong to criticize others if we first criticized ourselves, for if we first turned the searchlight on our own souls, we would never feel we had a right to turn it on the soul of anyone else. It is only because we are ignorant of our true condition that we fail to realize how badly we stand in need of pardon.

Have we ever offended God? Has He any right to be angry with us? Then why should we, who need pardon so badly, strive not to purchase it by pardoning others? The answer is because we never examine our own consciences.

We are so ignorant of our true condition that we know little more of ourselves than our name and address and how much we have; of our selfishness, our envy, our de-traction, our sin, we know absolutely nothing. In fact, in order that we may never know ourselves, we hate silence and solitariness. Lest our conscience should carry on with us an unbearable repartee, we drown out its voice in amusements, distractions, and noise. If we met ourselves in others, we would hate them.

If we knew ourselves better, we would be more forgiving of others. The harder we are on ourselves, the easier we will be on others. The man who has never learned to obey knows not how to command, and the man who has never disciplined himself knows not how to be merciful.

It is always the selfish who are unkind to others, and those who are hardest on themselves are the kindest to others, as the teacher who knows the least is always the most intolerant to his pupils.

Only a Lord who thought so little of Himself as to become man and die like a criminal could ever forgive the weakness of those who crucified Him.

It is not hatred that is wrong; it is hating the wrong thing that is wrong. It is not anger that is wrong; it is being angry at the wrong thing that is wrong. Tell me your enemy, and I will tell you what you are. Tell me your hatred, and I will tell you your character.

Do you hate religion? Then your conscience bothers you. Do you hate the wealthy? Then you are avaricious, and you want to be wealthy. Do you hate the common worker? Then you are selfish and a snob. Do you hate sin? Then you love God. Do you hate your hate, your selfishness, your quick temper, your wickedness? Then you are a good soul, for "If any man come to me . . . and hate not his own life, he cannot be my disciple."[10]

The second lesson to be derived from this First Word from the Cross is that there is no limit to pardon. Our Lord forgave when He was innocent and not because He Himself had been forgiven. Hence, we must forgive not only when we have been forgiven, but even when we are innocent.

The problem of the limits of pardon once troubled Peter, and he asked our Lord: "How often shall my brother offend against me, and I forgive him — till seven times?"[11] Peter thought he was stretching forgiveness by saying "seven times," for it was four more than the Jewish Masters enjoined.

Peter proposed a limit beyond which there was to be no forgiveness. He assumed the right to be forgiven is

[10] Luke 14:26.
[11] Matt. 18:21.

automatically renounced after seven offenses. It is equivalent to saying, "I renounce my right to collect debts from you if you never owe me more than seven dollars, but if you exceed that sum, then my duty of further cancellation ceases. I can throttle you for eight dollars."

Our Lord, in answering Peter, says that forgiveness has no limits; forgiveness is the surrender of all rights and the denial of limits. "I say not to thee till seven times but till seventy times seven."[12] That does not mean 490 literally, but infinitely. The Savior then proceeded to tell the parable of the unjust steward who, immediately after being forgiven by his lord a debt of ten thousand talents, choked a fellow servant who owed him a hundred pence. The unmerciful steward, by refusing to be merciful to his debtor, had his own mercy revoked. His guilt was not that, needing mercy, he refused to show it, but having received mercy, he was unmerciful still. "So also shall my heavenly Father do to you if you forgive not every one his brother."[13]

Forgive then, and we will be forgiven. Remit our anger against others, and God will remit His anger against us. Judgment is a harvest where we sow what we reap. If we

[12] Matt. 18:22.
[13] Matt. 18:35.

sowed anger against our brethren during life, we will reap the just anger of God. Judge not, and we shall not be judged.

If, during life, we forgive others from our hearts, on Judgment Day the all-wise God will permit something very unusual to Himself: He will forget how to add and will know only how to subtract. He who has a memory from all eternity will no longer remember our sins. Thus, we will be saved once again through divine "ignorance."

If we forgive others on the ground that they know not what they do, our Lord will forgive us on the ground that He no longer remembers what we did. It may well be that if He looks on a hand that now, after hearing the first Word on the Cross, gives a kindly blessing to an enemy, He will even forget that it was once a clenched fist red with the blood of Christendom.

> "And dars't thou venture still to live in sin,
> And crucify thy dying Lord again?
> Were not His pangs sufficient? Must He bleed
> Yet more? Oh, must our sinful pleasures feed
> Upon His torments, and augment the story
> Of the sad Passion of the Lord of glory!
> Is there no pity? Is there no remorse

In human breasts? Is there a firm divorce
Betwixt all mercy and the hearts of men?
Parted forever — ne'er to meet again?
No mercy bides with us: 'tis Thou alone,
Hast it, sweet Jesu, for us, that have none
For Thee: thou hast forestall'd our markets so
That all's above, and we have none below:
Nay, blessed Lord, we have not wherewithal
To serve our shiftless selves: unless we call To
    Thee,
Thou art our Savior, and hast power
To give, and whom we crucify each hour:
We are cruel, Lord, to Thee, and ourselves
    too;
Jesu forgive us; we know not what we do."

Francis Quarles

Second Word

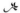

Envy

"This day thou shalt
be with me in Paradise."

Luke 23:43

Envy is sadness at another's good, and joy at another's
evil. What rust is to iron, what moths are to wool, what
termites are to wood, that envy is to the soul — the assas-
sination of brotherly love.

We are not here concerned with just envy or zeal,
which inspires us to emulate good example and to pro-
gress with those who are our betters, for the Scriptures en-
join us to "be zealous for spiritual gifts."[14] Rather, we here
touch on that sinful envy which is a willful grieving at another's good, either spiritual or temporal, for the reason

[14] 1 Cor. 14:1.

that it seems to diminish our own good. The honor paid to another is regarded by the envious man as a reflected disgrace on himself, and he is sad in consequence. Envy manifests itself in discord, hatred, malicious joy, backbiting, detraction, imputing of evil motives, jealousy, and calumny.

A sample of this kind of envy we find in one of the two women who asked Solomon to adjudicate their dispute. The first woman said, "I and this woman dwelt in one house. . . . And this woman's child died in the night: for in her sleep, she overlaid him. And rising in the dead time of the night, she took my child from my side, while I, thy handmaid, was asleep . . . and laid her dead child in my bosom." To which the other woman answered: "It is not so as thou sayest, but thy child is dead, and mine is alive."[15]

Since there were no witnesses, Solomon ordered a sword to be brought to him, for he rightly judged that the motherly heart of the real mother would rather give up her child than see him killed. Brandishing the glittering sword, he said, "Divide the living child in two, and give half to the one, and half to the other." Hearing this, the woman whose child was alive cried out in terror and pity,

[15] 3 Kings 3:17, 19-20, 22 (RSV = 1 Kings 3:17, 19-20, 22).

"I beseech thee, my lord, give her the child alive, and do not kill it." But the other said, "Let it be neither mine nor thine, but divide it."[16]

Then the king commanded the child be given to her who would rather give him up to another than have him killed, knowing that she must be the mother. The point of the story is that envy which is so jealous of the good of another may reach a point where it scruples not to take a life.

In our times, envy has taken on an economic form. The avarice of the rich is being matched by the envy of the poor. Some poor hate the rich, not because they have unjustly stolen their possessions, but because they *want* their possessions. Certain have-nots are scandalized at the wealth of the haves, only because they are tempted by lust for their possessions. They envy the rich, not because of their need, but because of their greed.

Combined with this is social envy or snobbery, which sneers at the higher position of others, because the snobs want to sit in their chairs and enjoy their applause. They assume that, in not arriving at such popular favor themselves, they were deprived of their due. That is why we

[16] 3 Kings 3:25-26 (RSV = 1 Kings 3:25-26).

hate those who do not pay sufficient attention to us and why we love those who flatter us.

If envy is on the increase today, as it undoubtedly is, it is because of the surrender of the belief of a future life and righteous divine justice. If this life is all, they think they should have all. From that point on, envy of others becomes their rule of life.

Our Lord was unceasing in His preaching against envy. To those who were envious of the mercy extended to lost sheep, He pictured the angels of Heaven rejoicing more at the one sinner doing penance than at the ninety-nine just who needed not penance.[17] To those who were envious of wealth He warned, "Lay not up to yourselves treasures on earth, where the rust and moth consume, and where thieves break through and steal. But lay up to yourselves treasures in Heaven, where neither the rust nor moth consume and where thieves do not break through, nor steal."[18]

When He encountered those who were envious of power, such as the Apostles quarreling about first place, He placed a child in the midst of them and, "putting His

[17] Luke 15:7.
[18] Matt. 6:19-20.

arms around him," reminded them that Heaven was open only to those who were as simple children, for Christ is not in the great but in the little: "Whosoever shall receive one such child as this in my name, receiveth me. And whosoever shall receive me, receiveth not me, but him that sent me."[19]

But Christ's preaching against envy did not save Him from the envious. Pilate was envious of His power; Annas was envious of His innocence; Caiphas was envious of His popularity; Herod was envious of His moral superiority; the scribes and Pharisees were envious of His wisdom. Each of these had built his judgment seat of mock moral superiority from which to sentence Morality to the Cross. And in order that He might no longer be a person to be envied, they reputed Him with the wicked.

Born between an ox and an ass, they now crucify Him between two criminals. That was the last insult they could give Him. To the public eye, they created the impression that three thieves, and not two, were silhouetted against the sky. In a certain sense, it was true: two stole gold out of avarice; one stole hearts out of love. *Salvandus, Salvator,* and *Salvatus:* the thief who could have been saved; the

---

[19] Mark 9:36.

thief who was saved; and the Savior who saved them. The crosses spelled out the words *envy, mercy,* and *pity.*

The thief on the left envied the power our blessed Lord claimed. As the chief priests, scribes, and ancients ridiculed the Savior, sneering: "He saved others; Himself He cannot save," the thief on the left added to their revilings: "If Thou be Christ, save Thyself and us."[20] In other words: "If I had that power of Yours, that power You claim as the Messiah, I would use it differently than to hang helpless on a tree. I would step down from the Cross, smite my enemies, and prove what power really is."

Thus did envy reveal that if it had the gifts it envies in others, it would misuse them, as the thief on the left would have surrendered redemption from sin for release from a nail. In like manner, many in the world today who are envious of wealth would probably lose their souls if they had that wealth. Envy never thinks of responsibilities. Looking only to self, it misuses every gift that comes its way.

Pity has quite a different effect on the soul. The thief on the right had no envy of the Master's power, but only pity for the Master's sufferings. Rebuking his companion

[20] Matt. 27:42; Luke 23:39.

on the left, the good thief said, "Neither dost thou fear God, seeing thou art under the same condemnation? And we indeed, justly, for we receive the due reward of our deeds; but this Man hath done no evil."[21]

There was not a spark of envy in him. He wanted nothing in all the world, not even to be removed from tragic companioning with his cross. He was not envious of God's power, for God knows best what to do with His power. He was not envious of his fellowmen, for they had nothing worth giving.

So he threw himself upon Divine Providence and asked only for forgiveness: "Lord, remember me when Thou shalt come into Thy kingdom."[22] A dying man asked a dying Man for life; a man without possessions asked a poor Man for a kingdom; a thief at the door of death asked to die a thief and steal Paradise.

And because He envied nothing, He received all: "Amen, I say to thee, this day thou shalt be with me in Paradise."

One would have thought a saint would have been the first soul purchased over the counter of Calvary by the red

[21] Luke 23:40-41.
[22] Luke 23:42.

coins of redemption, but in the divine plan, it is a thief who steals that privilege and marches as the escort of the King of Kings into Paradise.

Two lessons are taught us by this Second Word from the Cross. The first is that envy is the source of our wrong judgments about others. The chances are that if we are envious of others, nine times out of ten we will misjudge their characters.

Because the thief on the left was envious of the power of our Lord, he misjudged Him and missed both the divinity of the Savior and his own salvation. He falsely argued that power should always be used the way he would have used it — namely, to turn nails into rosebuds, a cross into a throne, blood into royal purple, and the blades of grass on the hillside into bayonets of offensive steel.

No one in the history of the world ever came closer to Redemption, and yet no one ever missed it by so far. His envy made him ask for the wrong thing; he asked to be taken down when he should have asked to be taken up. It makes one think of how much the envy of Herod resulted in an equally false judgment: He massacred the Innocents because he thought the Infant King came to destroy an earthy kingdom, whereas He came only to announce a heavenly one.

So it is with us. Backbiting, calumny, and false judgments are all born of our envy. We say, "Oh, he is jealous," or "She is jealous"; but how do we know that he or she is jealous unless we ourselves have felt that way? How do we know others are acting proudly unless we know how pride asserts itself? Every envious word is based on a false judgment of our own moral superiority. To sit in judgment makes us feel that we are above those who are judged and more righteous and more innocent than they.

To accuse others is to say, "I am not like that." To be envious of others is to say, "You have stolen that which is mine." Envy of others' wealth has resulted in the gross misjudgment that the best way to do away with its abuse in the hands of the rich is to dispossess them violently, so that the dispossessors may, in their turn, enjoy its abuse.

Envy of others' political power has given rise to the erroneous philosophy that even governments may be overthrown if organized violence is strong enough to do so.

Envy thus becomes the denial of all justice and love. In individuals, it develops a cynicism that destroys all moral values, for, by bankrupting others, we ourselves become bankrupt. In groups, it produces a deceit that extends the glad hand of welcome to those who differ, only until they are strong enough to cut it off.

Victory Over Vice

Since envy is so rampant in the world today, it is extremely good counsel to disbelieve ninety-nine percent of the wicked statements we hear about others. Think of how much the thief on the right had to discount to arrive at the truth. He had to disbelieve the judgment of four envious judges, the raillery of envious scribes and ancients, the blasphemous utterances of curious onlookers who loved murders, and the envious taunts of the thief on the left, who was willing to lose his soul if only he could keep his fingers nimble for more thefts.

But if he had been envious of the Lord's power, he would never have been saved. He found peace by disbelieving the envious scandalmongers. Our peace is found in the same incredulity.

The chances are that there is a bit of jealousy, a bit of envy, behind every cutting remark and barbed whispering we hear about our neighbor. It is always good to remember that there are always more sticks under the tree that has the most apples. There should be some consolation for those who are so unjustly attacked to remember that it is a physical impossibility for any man to get ahead of us who stays behind to kick us.

A second lesson to be learned from this Second Word is that the only way to overcome envy is, like the thief on the right, to show pity. As Christians in good faith, we are all members of the Mystical Body of Christ and should therefore love one another as Christ has loved us.

If our arm suffers an injury, our whole body feels the pain. In like manner, if the Church in any part of the world suffers martyrdom, we should feel pity toward it as part of our body, and that pity should express itself in prayer and good works. Pity should be extended not only to those outside the Church who are living as if the earth never bore a Cross, but even to the enemies of the Church who would destroy even the shadow of the Cross. God is their judge, not we.

And as potential brothers of Christ, sons of a heavenly Father, and children of Mary, they must be worth our pity since they were worth the Savior's Blood.

Unfortunately, there are some who blame the Church for receiving great sinners into the Church on their deathbeds.

A few years ago, one who was generally believed to be a racketeer and murderer met death at the hands of his fellow criminals. A few minutes before his death, he asked to be received into the Church, was baptized, received First Communion, and was anointed and given the last blessing. Some who should have known better protested against the Church. Imagine! Envy at the salvation of a soul!

Victory Over Vice

Why not rather rejoice in God's mercy, for, after all, did he not belong to the same profession as the thief on the right — and why should not our Lord be just as anxious to save twentieth-century thieves as first-century thieves? They both have souls. It would seem that sinful envy of the salvation of a thief is a greater sin than thievery.

One thief was saved: therefore, let no one despair. One thief was lost: therefore, let no one presume.

Have pity, then, on the miserable, and divine mercy will be the reward for your pity. When the Pharisees accused our Lord of eating with publicans and sinners, He retorted by reiterating the necessity of mercy: "The healthy have no need of a physician, but the sick have. Now go and learn what this means: I will have mercy and not sacrifice. For I am not come to call the just, but sinners."[23]

One day a woman went to the saintly Father John Vianney, the Curé of Ars, in France, and said, "My husband has not been to the sacraments or to Mass for years. He has been unfaithful, wicked, and unjust. He has just fallen from a bridge and was drowned — a double death of body and soul." The Curé answered, "Madam, there is a

---

[23] Cf. Mark 2:17.

short distance between the bridge and the water, and it is that distance which forbids you to judge."

There was just that distance between the two crosses which saved the penitent thief. If the thief on the right had been self-righteous, he would have looked down on Jesus and lost his soul. But because he was conscious of his own sin, he left room for divine pardon.

And the answer of the Redeemer to his request proves that to the merciful, love is blind; for if we love God and our neighbor, who may even be our enemy, Divine Love will go blind, as it did for the thief on the right. Christ will no longer be able to see our faults, and that blindness will be for us the dawn of the vision of Love.

The Penitent Thief

> "Say, bold but blessed thief,
> That in a trice
> Slipped into paradise,
> And in plain day
> Stol'st Heaven away,
> What trick couldst thou invent
> To compass thy intent?
> What arms?
> What charms?"

Victory Over Vice

"Love and belief."
"Say, bold but blessed thief,
How couldst thou read
A crown upon that head?
What text, what gloss —
A kingdom and a Cross?
How couldst thou come to spy
God in a man to die?
What light?
What sight?"
"The sight of grief —"
"I sight to God His pain;
And by that sight
I saw the light,
Thus did my grief
Beget relief.
And take this rule from me,
Pity thou Him, He'll pity thee.
Use this,
Ne'er miss,
Heaven may be stolen again."

Anonymous

Third Word

࿋

Lust

"Woman, behold thy son;
behold thy mother."

John 19:26, 27

Lust is an inordinate love of the pleasures of the flesh. The important word here is *inordinate,* for it was Almighty God Himself who associated pleasure with the flesh. He attached pleasure to eating in order that we might not be remiss in nourishing and preserving our individual lives. He associated pleasure with the marital act in order that husband and wife might not be remiss in their social obligations to propagate mankind and raise children for the kingdom of God.

The pleasure becomes sinful at that point where, instead of using it as means, we begin to use it as an end. To eat for the sake of eating is a sin, because eating is a means to an end, which is health. Lust, in like manner, is selfishness or perverted love. It looks not so much to the good of the other, as to the pleasure of self. It breaks the glass that holds the wine; it breaks the lute to snare the music. It subordinates the other to self for the sake of pleasure. Denying the quality of "otherness," it seeks to make the other person care for us, but not to make us care for the other person.

We are living today in what might properly be called an era of carnality. As the appeal to the spiritual relaxes, the demands of the flesh increase. Living less for God, human nature begins to live only for self, for "no man can serve two masters; for either he will hate the one, and love the other, or he will sustain the one, and despise the other."[24]

Peculiar to this era of carnality is the tendency to equate the perpetuity of marriage with the fleshly pleasure, so that, when the pleasure ends, the bond is presumed to be automatically dissolved. In America, for example, there is more than one divorce for every two marriages — an indication of how much we have ceased to be a Christian nation and how much we have forgotten

[24] Matt. 6:24.

the words of our Lord: "What therefore God hath joined together, let no man put asunder."[25]

The regrettable aspect of it all is that, with this increased sin, there is a decreased *sense* of sin. Souls sin more, but think less about it. Like the sick who are so moribund that they have no desire to be better, sinners become so calloused that they have no yearning for redemption. Having lost their eyes, they no longer want to see; the only pleasure left to them in the end is to mock and sneer at those who do.

It is never the pure who say that chastity is impossible but only the impure. We judge others by ourselves, and attribute to others the vices from which we ourselves refuse to abstain.

Some reparation had to be made for the sin of lust that, in Old Testament times, became so hideous to God that He would have withheld the destruction of the cities of Sodom and Gomorrah could but ten just men have been found within their gates.

Our Lord began making reparation for it at the first moment of the Incarnation, for He chose to be born of a virgin.

[25] Matt. 19:6.

Victory Over Vice

Why did He choose to transcend the laws of nature? The answer is very simple. Original Sin has been propagated to every human being from Adam to this very hour, with the exception of our Lady. The prolongation of this taint in human nature takes place through the carnal act, of which man is the active principle, for man was the head of the human race. Every time there is generation of one human being by another, through the union of man and woman, there is the propagation of Original Sin.

The problem confronting the Second Person of the Blessed Trinity in becoming man was how to become man without at the same time becoming sinful man, that is, man-infected by the sin to which all flesh is heir? How to become man without inheriting Original Sin? He had to be a true man in order to suffer for man, but He could not be a sinful man if He were to redeem man from sin. How could He be both man and yet sinless?

He could be man by being born of a woman; He could be sinless man, without Original Sin, by dispensing with man as the active principle of generation — in other words, by being born of a virgin. Thus it was that when the angel Gabriel appeared to Mary and told her that she was to conceive the Messiah, whose name would be called Jesus, she answered: "How can this be done, because I know not man?"[26] She had made the vow of virginity, and she intended to keep it.

The angel answered that the conception of the Son of Man would take place without man, through the power of the Holy Spirit, who would overshadow her. Being assured of her continued virginity, she accepted the motherhood of God Incarnate. "Be it done unto me, according to thy word."[27]

So it was that reparation for sins of the flesh began the first moment of the Incarnation through the Virgin Birth. That same love He manifested for virginity in the beginning, He re-echoed in the first sermon of His public life: "Blessed are the clean of heart, for they shall see God."[28]

Later on, when some scribes and Pharisees sought to malign His good name, He challenged them to find anything impure in His life: "Which of you shall convince me of sin?"[29]

The final atonement and reparation is made on Calvary, where, in reparation for all the impure desires and

[26] Luke 1:34.

[27] Luke 1:38.

[28] Matt. 5:8.

[29] John 8:46.

thoughts of men, our Lord is crowned with thorns; where, in reparation for all the sins of shame, He is stripped of His garments; where, in reparation for all the lusts of the flesh, He is almost dispossessed of His flesh, for according to Sacred Scripture, the very bones of His Body could be numbered.[30]

We are so used to looking upon artistic crucifixes of ivory and the beautiful images in our prayer books, that we think of our blessed Lord as being whole on the Cross. The fact is that He made such reparation for sins of the flesh that His Body was torn, His Blood poured forth, and Scripture refers to Him on the Cross as a leper, as one struck by God and afflicted, so that "there is no beauty in Him, nor comeliness . . . that we should be desirous of Him."[31]

Our Lord chose to go even further in reparation for the sins of lust by dispossessing Himself of the two most legitimate claims of the flesh. If there was ever a pure and legitimate claim in the realm of the flesh, it is the claim to the love of one's own mother. If there is any honest title to affection in the universe of the flesh, it is the bonds of love that attach one to a fellowman. But the flesh was so

[30] Ps. 21:18 (RSV = Ps. 22:17).
[31] Isa. 53:2.

misused by man and so perverted that our divine Savior renounced even these legitimate bonds of the flesh in order to atone for the illegitimate.

He became totally un-fleshed, in order to atone for the abuse of the flesh, by giving away His Mother and His best friend. So, to His own Mother He looks and bids farewell: "Woman, behold thy son"; and to His best friend He looks and bids farewell again: "Behold thy mother."

How different from the world! A mother will deprive her son of an advanced education in a foreign land, saying, "I cannot give up my son." Or a wife will deprive her husband of good material advancement through a short absence, saying, "I cannot give up my husband." These are not the cries of noble love but of attachment. Our Lord did not say, "I cannot give up my Mother." He gave her up. He loved her enough to give her away for her life's plan and destiny — namely, to be *our* Mother.

Here was a love that was strong enough to forget itself, in order that others might never want for love. He made the sacrifice of His Mother so that we might have her. He wounded Himself like the pelican, so that we might be nourished by her motherhood. Mary accepted the poor exchange to carry out her Son's redemptive work. And at that moment when Jesus surrendered even the legitimate claims of the flesh and gave us His Mother, Mary, and His best friend, John, selfishness died its death.

Two lessons are to be learned from this Third Word from the Cross: that the only real escape from the demands of the flesh is to find something more than the flesh to love; and that Mary is the refuge of sinners.

If we could ever find anything we loved more than the flesh, the demands of the flesh would be less imperative. This is the "escape" a mother offers her boy when she says: "Don't do anything of which your mother would ever be ashamed." If there is that higher love of his mother, the boy will always have a consecrated sense of affection, something for which he will be willing to make sacrifices.

When a mother makes such an appeal to her son, she is merely echoing the lesson of the Savior, who, in giving His Mother to us as our Mother, equivalently said, "My children, never do anything of which your Mother would be ashamed." Let a soul but love that Mother, and he will love her divine Son, Jesus, who, in order to make satisfaction for the unlawful pleasure of the flesh, surrendered to us His last and lawful attachment — His Mother.

The psychology of this enthusiasm for a higher love of Jesus and Mary as an escape from the unlawful attachments of the flesh is this: by it, we avoid undue concentration on lower loves and their explosions. Think about your mouth for five minutes, and you will have an undue concentration of saliva. Think about your heart for five minutes, and you will believe you have heart trouble, although the chances are nine out of ten that you have not. Stand on a stage and think about your hands, and they will begin to feel as big as hams.

The balance and equilibrium of the whole system is disturbed when an organ is isolated from its function in the whole organism, or divorced from its higher purpose. People who are always talking, reading, and thinking about sex are like singers who think more about their larynx than about singing. They make that which is subordinate to a higher purpose so all-important that the harmony of life is upset.

But suppose that, instead of concentrating on an organ, one fitted that organ into a pattern of living; then all the uneasiness would end. The skilled orator never feels his hands are awkward because, being enthused about his speech, he makes his hands subordinate to their higher purpose.

Our Lord practically said the same thing: "Be not solicitous . . . what you shall eat." [32] So it is with the flesh.

[32] Matt. 6:25.

Victory Over Vice

Cultivate a higher love, a purpose of living, a goal of existence, a desire to correspond to all that God wants us to be, and the lower passion will be absorbed by it.

The Church applies this psychology to the vow of chastity. The Church asks her priests and nuns to surrender even the lawful pleasures of the flesh, not because she does not want them to love, but because she wants them to love better. She knows that their love for souls will be greater as their love for the flesh is less, just as our Lord died on the Cross for men because He loved His own life less.

Nor must it be thought that the vow of chastity is a burden. Thompson has called it a "passionless passion, a wild tranquility." And so it is. A new passion is born with the vow of chastity, the passion for the love of God. It is the consolation of that higher love which makes the surrender of the lower love so easy. And only when that higher love is lost does the vow begin to be a burden, just as honesty becomes a burden only to those who have lost the sense of others' rights.

The reason there is a degeneration in the moral order and a decay of decency is because men and women have lost the higher love. Ignoring Christ their Savior, who loved them unto the death on Calvary, and Mary who loved them unto becoming Queen of Martyrs beneath that Cross, they have nothing for which to make the sacrifice.

The only way love can be shown in this world is by sacrifice — namely, the surrender of one thing for another. Love is essentially bound up with choice, and choice is a negation, and negation is a sacrifice. When a young man sets his heart upon a young woman and asks her to marry him, he is not only saying "I choose you"; he is also saying "I do not choose, I reject, all others. I give them all up for you." Apply this to the problem of lust.

Take away all love above the flesh, take away God, the crucifix, the Sorrowful Mother, salvation, eternal happiness — and what possibility is there for choice? What is to be gained by denying the imperious and revolutionary demands of the flesh? But grant the divine, and the flesh's greatest joy is to throw itself on the altar of the one loved, where it counts its sorrow a cheap price for the blissful joy of giving.

Then its greatest despair is not to be needed; it could almost find it in its heart to inflict a wound that it might bind and heal. Such is the attitude of the pure. They have integrated their flesh with the divine; they have sublimated its cravings with the Cross. Having a higher love, they now make the surrender of the lower, so that their Mother may never be put to shame.

Mary is the refuge of sinners. She who is the Virgin Most Pure is also the Refuge of Sinners. She knows what sin is, not by the experience of its falls, not by tasting its bitter regrets, but by seeing what it did to her divine Son.

She looked upon His torn and bleeding flesh hanging from Him like rays of a purple sunset, and she came to know how much flesh sinned by seeing what His flesh suffered. What better way in all the world was there to measure the heinousness of sin than by seeing, when left alone with Him for three hours, what it could do to Innocence and Purity.

She is the Refuge of Sinners not only because she knows sin through Calvary, but also because she chose, during the most terrifying hours of her life, a converted sinner as her companion. The measure of our appreciation of friends is our desire to have them around us in the moment of our greatest need.

Mary heard Jesus say, "The harlots and publicans will enter the kingdom of Heaven before the scribes and Pharisees."[33] So she chose the absolved harlot, Magdalen, as her

[33] Cf. Matt. 21:31.

companion at the Cross. What the scandalmongers of that day must have said when they saw our Blessed Mother in the company of a woman who everyone knew was the kind who sold her body without giving away her soul.

Magdalen knew that day why Mary is the Refuge of Sinners, and certainly our day, too, can learn that if she had Magdalen as a companion then, she is willing to have us as companions now.

Mary's purity is not a holier-than-thou purity, a stand-offish holiness that gathers up its robes lest they be stained by the sinful; nor is it a despising purity that looks down upon the impure. Rather, it is a radiating purity that is no more spoiled by solicitude for the fallen than a ray of sunshine is sullied by a dirty windowpane through which it pours.

There is no reason for the fallen to be discouraged. Hope is the message of Golgotha. Find a higher love than the flesh, a love pure, understanding, and redeeming, and the struggle will be easy. That higher love is on the Cross and beneath it.

We almost seem to forget that there is a Cross at all. He begins to look more like a red rose, and she begins to look like the stem. That stem reaches down from Calvary into all our wounded hearts of earth, sucking up our prayers and petitions and conveying them to Him. That is why roses have thorns in this life — to keep away every disturbing influence that might destroy our union with Jesus and Mary.

Acknowledgment

If Christ should come on earth some summer day
And walk unknown upon our busy street
I wonder how 'twould be if we should meet,
And being God — if He would act that way.

Perhaps the kindest thing that He would do
Would be just to forget I failed to pray
And clasp my hand, forgivingly, and say,
"My child, I've heard my Mother speak of you."

Mrs. Frederick V. Murphy

Fourth Word

જ⁄

Pride

"My God, my God, why
hast Thou forsaken me?"

Matthew 27:46

Pride is an inordinate love of one's own excellence, either
of body or mind or the unlawful pleasure we derive from
thinking we have no superiors. Pride being swollen egoism,
it erects the human soul into a separate center of origin
apart from God, exaggerates its own importance, and becomes a world in and for itself.

All other sins are evil deeds, but pride insinuates itself even unto good works to destroy and slay them. For
that reason, Sacred Scriptures says, "Pride goeth before
destruction."[34]

[34] Prov. 16:18.

Victory Over Vice

Pride manifests itself in many forms: atheism, which is a denial of our dependence on God, our Creator and our final end; intellectual vanity, which makes minds un-teachable because they think they know all there is to know; superficiality, which judges others by their clothes, their accent, and their bank account; snobbery, which sneers at inferiors as the earmark of its own superiority, "they are not of our set"; vainglory, which prompts some Catholic parents to refuse to send their boys and girls to Catholic colleges, because they would there associate only with the children of carpenters; presumptuousness, which inclines a man to seek honors and positions quite beyond his capacity; and exaggerated sensitiveness, which makes one incapable of moral improvements because of unwillingness to hear one's own faults.

Pride it was that made Satan fall from Heaven and man fall from grace. By its very nature, such undue self-exaltation could be cured only by self-humiliation. That is why He who might have been born in a palace by the Tiber, as befitting His majesty as the Son of God, chose to appear before men in a stable as a child wrapped in swad-dling bands.

Added to this humility of His birth was the humility of His profession — a carpenter in an obscure village of

Nazareth whose name was a reproach among the great. Just as today there are those who sneer at the humble walks of life, so, too, there were then those who sneered: "Is not this the carpenter's son?"[35] There was also the humility of His actions, for never once did He work a miracle in His own behalf, not even to supply Himself with a place to lay His head.

Humility of example there was, too, when, on Holy Thursday night, He who is the Lord of Heaven and earth, girds Himself with a towel, gets down on His knees, and, with basin and water, washes the twenty-four calloused feet of His Apostles saying, "The servant is not greater than his lord. . . . If, then, I, being your Lord and Master have washed your feet, you also ought to wash one another's feet."[36]

Finally, there was humility of precept: "Unless you be converted, and become as little children, you shall not enter into the kingdom of Heaven."[37]

But the supreme humiliation of all was the manner of death He chose, for "He humbled Himself . . . even to the

---

[35] Matt. 13:55.
[36] Cf. John 13:14, 16.
[37] Matt. 18:3.

death of the cross."[38] To atone for false pride of ancestry, He thrusts aside the consolation of divinity; for pride of popularity, He is laughed to scorn as He hangs cursed upon a tree; for pride of snobbery, He is put in the company of thieves; for pride of wealth, He is denied even the ownership of His own deathbed; for pride of flesh, He was scourged until "there was no beauty in Him"; for pride in influential friends, He is forgotten even by those whom He cured; for pride of power, He is weak and abandoned; for pride of those who surrender God and their Faith, He wills to feel without God.

For all the egotism, false independence, and atheism, He now offers satisfaction by surrendering the joys and consolations of His divine nature. Because proud men forgot God, He permits Himself to feel Godlessness, and it breaks His heart in the saddest of all cries: "My God, my God, why hast thou forsaken me?" There is union even in the separation; but they are words of desolation uttered that we might never be without consolation.

Two lessons emerge from this word: glory not in ourselves, for God resists the proud; and glory in humility, for humility is truth and the path to true greatness.

[38] Phil. 2:8.

Why should we be proud? As St. Paul reminds us, "What hast thou that thou hast not received? And if thou hast received, why dost thou glory, as if thou hadst not received it?"[39] Is it our voice, our wealth, our beauty, our talents of which we are proud? But what are these but gifts of God, any one of which He might revoke this second?

From a material point of view, we are worth so little. The content of a human body is equivalent to as much iron as there is in a nail, as much sugar as there is in two lumps, as much oil as there is in seven bars of soap, as much phosphorus as there is in 2,200 matches, and as much magnesium as it takes to develop one photograph. In all, the human body, chemically, is worth just a few dollars. "Oh, why should the spirit of mortal be proud?"

But *spiritually* we are worth more than the universe: "For what shall it profit a man, if he gains the whole world, and suffer the loss of his soul? Or what shall a man give in exchange for his soul?"[40]

God resists the proud. The Pharisee who praised his own good deeds in the forefront of the Temple is condemned; the poor publican in the rear of the Temple, who

[39] 1 Cor. 4:7.
[40] Mark 8:36-37.

calls himself a sinner and strikes his breast in a plea for pardon, goes to his house justified. The harlots and the publicans who are conscious of their sin enter the kingdom of Heaven before the scribes and the Pharisees, who are conscious of their righteousness.

The heavenly Father is thanked for concealing His wisdom from the self-wise and the conscious intellectuals and for revealing it to the simple: "I confess to thee, O Father, Lord of Heaven and earth, because Thou hast hidden these things from the wise and prudent, and hast revealed them to little ones."[41]

Surely anyone who has had experience with the proud will bear witness to the truth of this statement: If my own eternal salvation were conditioned upon saving the soul of one self-wise man who prided himself on his learning, or one hundred of the most morally corrupt men and women of the streets, I would choose the easier task of converting the hundred. Nothing is more difficult to conquer in all the world than intellectual pride. If battleships could be lined with it instead of with armor, no shell could ever pierce it.

This is easy to understand, for if a man thinks he knows it all, there is nothing left for him to know, not

---

[41] Luke 10:21.

even what God might tell him. If the soul is filled to the brim with the ego, there is no place left for God. If a vessel is filled with water, it cannot also be filled with oil. So it is with the soul.

God can give His truth and life only to those who have emptied themselves. We must create a vacuum in our own souls to make room for grace. We live under the impression that we do more than we actually do. Take, for example, the simple fact of drinking liquid through a straw. We erroneously believe that we draw up the liquid through the straw. We do not, for, strictly speaking, there is no such thing as suction. All that we do is create a vacuum; the atmosphere presses down on the liquid with a weight equal to that of an ocean covering the earth to a depth of thirty-four feet. It is this pressure that pushes the liquid up through the straw when we create the vacuum.

So, too, in our spiritual lives. The good we accomplish is not through the action of ourselves, as much as it is through the spiritual pressure of God's grace. All we have to do is create a vacuum, to count ourselves as nothing — and immediately God fills the soul with His power and truth.

The paradox of apostolate, then, is this: the less we think we are, the more good we do. It was only when Peter had labored all night and taken nothing, that our Lord filled his boat with the miraculous draught of fishes. The higher the building, the deeper the foundation; the greater the virtue, the more the humility.

God's instruments for good in the world are, for that reason, only the humble. Reducing themselves to zero, they leave room for infinity, whereas those who think themselves infinite, God leaves with their little zero.

Even in the world we find a natural basis for humility. As long as we are small, everything else seems big. A boy mounts a broomstick that is no more than four feet long, yet to him it is a Pegasus traveling through space; he can hear the hoofs beating the clouds as he clings to the "whistling mane of every wind."[42] His world is peopled with giants because he is so little; tin soldiers to him are real soldiers fighting real battles, and the red of the carpet is the blood of the battlefield.

When he grows to be a big man, the giants shrink in size; the horses become broomsticks, and the soldiers are painted tin no more than three inches high. In the spiritual order, it is the same; as long as there is a God who is wiser than we, greater than we, more powerful than we, then the world is a house of wonders.

[42] Francis Thompson, "The Hound of Heaven."

Truth, then, is something so vast that not even an eternity can sound its depths. Love, then, is so abiding that not even Heaven can dull its ecstasies. Goodness becomes so profound that thanks must ever be on one's lips.

But just forget God, make yourself a god, and then your little learning is your title to omniscience. Then the saints become for you stupid fools; the martyrs, "fanatics"; the religious, "dumb"; Confession, a "priestly invention"; the Eucharist, a "vestige of paganism"; Heaven, a "childish fancy"; and truth, a "delusion." It must be wonderful to know so much, but it must be terrible to find out in the end that one really knows so little.

The second lesson to be derived from this Fourth Word from the Cross is that humility is truth. Humility is not an underestimation of our talents or gifts or powers, nor is it their exaggeration. A man who is six feet tall is not humble if he says he is only five feet four inches tall, just as he is not humble if he says he is seven feet tall. Humility is truth, or the recognition of gifts as gifts, faults as faults. Humility is dependence on God, as pride is independence of Him.

It was that sense of independence or being without God which wrung out of the heart of our Lord on the Cross this pitiable cry of abandonment: "My God, my

God, why hast Thou forsaken me?" The humble soul, conscious of his dependence on God, is always the thankful soul.

How many singers, orators, musicians, actors, doctors, and professors ever think of thanking God for the special talents that made them outstanding in their profession? Out of the ten lepers who were made clean, only one returned to give thanks. "Were not ten made clean? And where are the nine?"[43] probably represents the proportion of the ungrateful who thank not because they are not humble.

The humble soul will always avoid praising his own good works and thus making void the virtues of his deeds. Self-praise devours merit; and those who have done good things to be seen by men, and who trumpet their philanthropies in the marketplaces, will one day hear the saddest words of tongue or pen: "Thou hast already had thy reward."[44]

The humble man, even if he is great in the world's eyes, will esteem himself less than others, for he will always suspect that their internal greatness may far overreach his

[43] Luke 17:17.
[44] Cf. Matt. 6:2.

insignificant external greatness. He will therefore not flaunt his accidental superiority before his fellowman, for to do so is to prove one is not truly great. The really big men are the humble men; they are always approachable, kind, and understanding.

It is the little men who must put on airs. The rich boy need not wear good clothes to impress his friends with his wealth, but the poor boy must do so to create the false impression of wealth. So it is with those who have nothing in their heads; they must be eternally creating the impression of how much they know, the books they have read, and the university from which they graduated.

The learned man never has to "seem" learned, as the saint never has to appear pious — but the hypocrite does. The fact that so many men take honors seriously, change their voices, and cultivate poses, proves they never should have had the honors; the honors were too big for them. They could not assimilate the honors; rather, the honors assimilated them. Instead of wearing the purple, the purple wears them.

A sponge can absorb so much water and no more; a character can absorb so much praise and no more; the point of saturation is reached when the honor ceases to be a part of him and begins to stick out like a sore thumb.

Victory Over Vice

The truly great are like St. Philip Neri,[45] who one day, seeing a criminal being led off to prison, said: "There goes Philip Neri, except for the grace of God."

Suppose we began to be humble and esteemed others at least no less than ourselves. Suppose to those who wounded us with their slanderous darts, we answered, "Father, forgive!" Suppose to those who classified us with thieves, we made the best of it and converted them saying, "This day, Paradise." Suppose out of those who shamed us before relatives, as Jesus was shamed before His Mother, we made a new friend for our heavenly Mother: "Behold thy son!" Suppose to those beneath us in worldly dignity, we humbled ourselves and asked them for a drink: "I thirst!"

Suppose we began to be truthful, and estimated ourselves at our real worth. If we did these things for but one hour, we would completely revolutionize the world. We are not wanting an example, for we have before our eyes Him who humbled Himself to the death on the Cross, who surrendered divine consolation as power put on the rags of weakness and strength girded itself in abandonment, and, being God, appeared to be without God.

---

[45] St. Philip Neri (1515-1595), founder of the Congregation of the Oratory.

And why did He do this? Because we have been trying to lead our lives without God — to be independent. By choosing the humiliation of the Cross in reparation for pride, He takes us back again to the story of David and Goliath.

Goliath was a great giant clothed in an armor of steel and carrying in his hand a mighty sword. David was the shepherd boy without defensive steel and carrying no other weapon than a staff, and five little stones from a nearby brook. Goliath scorned him, saying, "Am I a dog, that thou comest to me with a staff?" David answered, humbly, not trusting in his own power, "I come to thee in the name of the Lord."[46] The outcome we know. The boy with a stone killed the giant with the armor and sword.

The victory of David symbolized the reality of Good Friday. Pride is Goliath. Our Lord is the humble David who comes to slay pride with the staff of His Cross and five little stones — five wounds, in hands, feet, and side. With no other weapon than these five wounds and the staff of the Cross do we gain victories over the Goliath of pride on the battlefield of our soul.

[46] 1 Kings 17:43, 45 (RSV = 1 Sam. 17:43, 45).

Victory Over Vice

To the worldly they seem ill-fitted for battle, and impotent to conquer, but not if we understand God's plan from the beginning: "The foolish things of the world hath God chosen, that he may confound the wise; and the weak things of the world hath God chosen that he may confound the strong."[47] It was with a Cross and a crowned brow that God won the day.

As Oscar Wilde puts it:

> O smitten mouth! O forehead crowned with
>   thorn!
> O chalice of all common miseries!
>
> Thou for our sakes that loved Thee not has borne
> An agony of endless centuries,
> And we were vain and ignorant nor knew
> That when we stabbed Thy heart it was our own
>   real hearts we slew.
>
> Being ourselves the sowers and the seeds,
> The night that covers and the lights that fade,
> The spear that pierces and the side that bleeds,
> The lips betraying and the life betrayed;

[47] 1 Cor. 1:27.

Pride

The deep hath calm: the moon hath rest: but we
Lords of the natural world are yet our own dread
    enemy.

Nay, nay, we are but crucified, and though
The bloody sweat falls from our brows like rain,
Loosen the nails — we shall come down I know,
Stanch the red wounds — we shall be whole again,
No need have we of hyssop-laden rod,
That which is purely human, that is Godlike,
    that is God.

The Fifth Word

Gluttony

"I thirst."

John 19:28

Gluttony is an inordinate indulgence in food or drink, either in taking more than is necessary, in taking it at the wrong time, or in taking it too luxuriously. It is sinful because reason demands that food and drink be taken for the necessities and conveniences of nature, not for pleasure alone.

The Gospel describes Dives as being guilty of this sin. There is no mention that Dives was a wicked man. We have no record of him underpaying his servants or of being guilty of any moral turpitude. Our Lord tells us only that he was "clothed in purple and fine linen; and feasted sumptuously every day."[48]

---

[48] Luke 16:19.

Victory Over Vice

And there was a certain beggar named Lazarus, who lay at his gate, full of sores, desiring to be filled with the crumbs that fell from the rich man's table, and no one did give him; moreover, the dogs came and licked his sores. And it came to pass that the beggar died and was carried by the angels into Abraham's bosom. And the rich man also died, and he was buried in hell. And lifting up his eyes when he was in torments, he saw Abraham afar off, and Lazarus in his bosom. And he cried and said: "Father Abraham, have mercy on me, and send Lazarus, that he may dip the tip of his finger in water, to cool my tongue; for I am tormented in this flame."

And Abraham said to him: "Son, remember that thou didst receive good things in thy lifetime, and likewise Lazarus evil things, but now he is comforted; and thou art tormented. And besides all this, between us and you, there is fixed a great chaos, so that they who would pass from hence to you, cannot, nor from thence come hither."

And he said, "Then, father, I beseech thee that thou wouldst send him to my father's house, for I have five brethren, that he may testify unto them, lest they also come into this place of torments."

And Abraham said to him, "They have Moses and the prophets; let them hear them." But he said, "No, father Abraham; but if one went to them from the dead, they will do penance." And he said to him, "If they hear not Moses and the prophets, neither will they believe, if one rise again from the dead."[49]

If there is any indication of the present degeneration of society better than another, it is the excess of luxury in the modern world. When men begin to forget their souls, they begin to take great care of their bodies. There are more athletic clubs in the modern world than there are spiritual retreat houses; and who shall count the millions spent in beauty shops to glorify faces that will one day be the prey of worms?

It is not particularly difficult to find thousands who will spend two or three hours a day in exercising, but if you ask them to bend their knees to God in five minutes of prayer, they protest that it is too long. Added to this is the shocking amount that is yearly spent, not in the normal pleasure of drinking, but in its excess.

[49] Luke 16:20-31.

Victory Over Vice

The scandal increases when one considers the necessary wants of the poor which could have been supplied by the amount spent for such dehumanization. The divine judgment upon Dives is bound to be repeated upon many of our generation, who will find that the beggars for whose service they refused to interrupt their luxuries will be seated at the banquet of the King of Kings, while they, like Dives, will be the beggars for but a drop of water.

Some reparation had to be made for gluttony, drunkenness, and excessive luxury. That reparation began at the birth of our Lord, when He who might have pulled down the heavens for His housetop and the stars for His chandeliers, chose to be rejected by men and driven as an outcast to a cave in the hillsides of the least of the cities of Israel.

The very first sermon He preached was a plea for detachment: "Blessed are the poor in spirit, for theirs is the kingdom of Heaven."[50] He began His public life by fasting forty days and bade men, "Be not solicitous for your life, what you shall eat, nor for your body, what you shall put on."[51]

[50] Matt. 5:3.
[51] Matt. 6:25.

Traveling about as an itinerant prophet, He admitted He was as homeless as at His birth and that the beasts and birds had a better habitation than He: "The foxes have holes, and the birds of the air, nests; but the Son of Man hath not where to lay His head."[52]

There was no luxury in the way He dined, for we know of but one meal that He himself prepared, and it consisted only of bread and fish.[53]

Finally, at the Cross, He is stripped of His garments and denied a deathbed, in order to go out of His own world as He came into it: Lord of it and yet possessing nothing. The waters of the sea were His, and all the fountains of the earth had sprung up at His word; He it was who drew the bolt of nature's waterfalls and shut up the seas with doors; He it was who said, "Whosoever drinketh of this water shall thirst again; but he that shall drink of the water that I will give him shall not thirst forever. If any man thirst, let him come to me, and drink."[54]

But now He lets fall from His lips the shortest of the seven cries from the Cross and the one that expresses the

---

[52] Matt. 8:20.
[53] John 21:9-10, 12.
[54] John 4:13; 7:37.

keenest of all human sufferings in reparation for those who have had their fill: "I thirst."

A soldier immediately put a sponge full of vinegar on a stick and pressed it to His mouth. Thus was fulfilled the prophecy uttered by the psalmist a thousand years before: "In my thirst they gave me vinegar to drink."[55]

He who fed the birds of the air is left unfed; He who changed water into wine now thirsts; the everlasting fountains are dry; the God-man is poverty-stricken. The divine "Lazarus" stands at the world's door and begs for a crumb and a drop, but the door of generosity is closed in His face.

Thus was reparation made for the luxury of eating and drinking. When Mirabeau was dying, he called for opium, saying, "You promised to spare me needless suffering. . . . Support this head, the greatest head in France." When Christ is dying, He refuses the drug to alleviate His suffering.[56] He deliberately wills to feel the most poignant of human wants, so that He might balance in the scales of justice those who had more than they needed.

He even made Himself the least of all men by asking them for a drink — not a drink of earthly water. That is

[55] Ps. 68:22 (RSV = Ps. 69:21).
[56] Mark 15:23.

not what He wanted, but a drink for His thirsty heart — a drink of love: I thirst for love.

This word from the Cross reveals that there is a double hunger and a double thirst: one of the body, the other of the soul. On many previous occasions, our Lord had distinguished between them: "Woe to you that are filled, for you shall hunger. Woe to you that now laugh, for you shall mourn and weep." "Blessed are ye that hunger now, for you shall be filled. Blessed are ye that weep now, for you shall laugh."[57]

Then to the multitude who followed Him across the sea in search of bread, He said: "Labor not for the meat which perisheth, but for that which endureth unto life everlasting, which the Son of Man will give you."[58]

To the Samaritan woman who came to draw water at Jacob's well, He foretold, "Whosoever drinketh of this water shall thirst again; but he that shall drink of the water that I will give him shall not thirst forever. But the water that I will give him shall become in him a fountain of water, springing up into life everlasting."[59]

---

[57] Luke 6:21, 25.
[58] John 6:27.
[59] John 4:13-14.

But above all other references to the food and drink of the inner man as contrasted with that of the outer man, He promised the supreme nourishment of Himself: "For my flesh is meat indeed, and my blood is drink indeed."[60]

In the light of this double hunger and thirst of body and soul, the distinction between dieting and fasting becomes clear. The Church fasts; the world diets. Materially there is no difference, for a person can lose twenty pounds one way as well as the other. The difference is in the intention.

The Christian fasts not for the sake of the body, but for the sake of the soul; the pagan fasts not for the sake of the soul, but for the sake of the body. The Christian does not fast because he believes the body is wicked, but in order to make it pliable in the hands of the soul, like a tool in the hands of a skilled workman.

That brings us down to the basic problem of life. Is the soul the tool of the body, or the body the tool of the soul? Should the soul do what the body wants, or should the body do what the soul wants? Each has its appetites, and each is imperious in the satisfaction of its wants. If we please one, we displease the other, and vice versa. Both of them cannot sit down together at the banquet of life.

[60] John 6:56 (RSV = John 6:55).

Gluttony

The development of character depends on which hunger and thirst we cultivate. To diet or to fast — that is the problem. To lose a double chin in order to be more beautiful in the eyes of creatures or to lose it in order to keep the body tamed and ever obedient to the spiritual demands of the soul — that is the question. Human worth can be judged by human desires.

Tell me your hungers and your thirsts, and I will tell you what you are. Do you hunger for money more than for mercy, for riches more than for virtue, and for power more than for service? Then you are selfish, pampered, and proud. Do you thirst for the wine of everlasting life more than for pleasure, and for the poor more than for the favor of the rich, and for souls more than for the first places at table? Then you are a humble Christian.

The great pity is that so many have been so concerned with the body that they neglect the soul, and in neglecting the soul, they lose the appetite for the spiritual. Just as it is possible in the physiological order for a man to lose all appetite for food, so it is possible in the spiritual order to lose all desire for the supernatural. Gluttonous about the perishable, they become indifferent to the everlasting.

Like deaf ears, which are dead to the environment of harmony, and blind eyes, which are dead to the environment of beauty, so warped souls become dead to the environment of the divine.

Darwin tells us in his autobiography that, in his love for the biological, he lost all the taste he once had for poetry and music, and he regretted the loss all the days of his life. Nothing so much dulls the capacity for the spiritual as excessive dedication to the material.

Excessive love of money destroys a sense of value; excessive love of the flesh kills the values of the spirit. Then comes a moment when everything seems to rebel against the higher law of our being. As the poet has put it, "All things betrayest thee, who betrayest me." Nature is so loyal to its Maker that it is always in the end disloyal to those who abuse it. "Traitorous trueness and loyal deceit" is its best poetic description, for in faithfulness to Him it will always be fickle with us.

The Fifth Word from the Cross is God's plea to the human heart to satisfy itself at the only satisfying fountains. God cannot compel men to thirst for the holy in place of the base, or for the divine rather than the secular. That is why His plea is merely an affirmation: "I thirst," meaning, "I thirst to be thirsted for." And His thirst is our salvation.

A twofold recommendation is hidden in this short sermon from the Cross: first, to mortify bodily hunger and thirst, and second, to cultivate a spiritual hunger and thirst.

We are to mortify bodily hunger and thirst, not because the flesh is wicked, but because the soul must ever exercise mastery over it, lest it become a tyrant. Quite apart from avoiding all excesses, the Cross commits us even to the minimizing of expenditures for luxuries, for the sake of the poor. How many ever think of forgoing an elaborate dinner and theater party, or a debut, out of genuine sympathy and affection for Christ's poor? Dives did not, and he lost his soul because of that forgetfulness. How many, in less ample circumstances, even mortify themselves one movie a month in order to drop its equivalent in the poor box, that He who sees in secret may reward in secret?

The divine counsel concerning such restraint of bodily appetites is unmistakable. On one occasion, when our Lord was invited to the home of the prince of the Pharisees, He addressed the host himself saying, "When thou makest a dinner or a supper, call not thy friends, nor thy brethren, nor thy kinsmen, nor thy neighbors who are rich; lest perhaps they also invite thee again, and a recompense be made to thee. But when thou makest a feast, call the poor, the maimed, the lame, and the blind. And thou shalt be blessed, because they have not wherewith to make thee recompense; for recompense shall be made thee at the resurrection of the just."[61]

The money we spend in the excesses of bodily hunger and thirst will do us no good on the last day; but the poor whom we have assisted by our restraint and mortification will stand up as so many advocates before the bar of divine justice and will plead for mercy on our souls, even though they once were heavily laden with sin.

The heavenly Judge cannot be bought with money, but He can be swayed by the poor. On that last day — the only one that really counts — will be fulfilled the beautifully prophetic words of the Mother of our Lord: "He hath filled the hungry with good things; and the rich he hath sent empty away."[62]

When such surrenders of the superfluous food and drink are made for the soul's sake, let it all be done in a spirit of joy. "And when you fast, be not as the hypocrites, sad. For they disfigure their faces, that they may appear unto men to fast. Amen, I say to you, they have received their reward. But thou, when thou fastest, anoint thy head, and wash thy face; that thou appear not to men to

[61] Luke 14:12-14.
[62] Luke 1:53.

fast, but to thy Father who is in secret; and thy Father who seeth in secret, will repay thee."[63]

We are, in addition, to cultivate a spiritual hunger and thirst. Mortification of the bodily appetites is only a means, not an end. The end is union with God, the soul's desire. "Taste and see that the Lord is sweet."[64] The great tragedy of life is not so much what men have suffered, but what they have missed. It comes within the compass of a few to satisfy their earthly desires with wealth, but there is no man living, who, if he willed it, could not enjoy the spiritual food and drink that God serves to all who ask.

And yet how few there are who ever think of nourishing their souls. How few there must have been in Jerusalem to have drawn from our Lord the sweet complaint: "How often would I have gathered together thy children, as the hen doth gather her chickens under her wings, and thou wouldst not?"[65]

Well indeed might the Savior say to us, as we listen to the cry "I thirst," the words he addressed to the woman at the well: "If thou didst know the gift of God, and who He

[63] Matt. 6:16-18.
[64] Ps. 33:9 (RSV = Ps. 34:8).
[65] Matt. 23:37.

is that saith to thee, 'Give me to drink'; thou perhaps wouldst have asked of Him, and He would have given thee living water."[66]

But how many ask? Consider the greatest gift of God to men: the Bread of Life. How few avail themselves of the divine presence to break their fast each morning on the heavenly food of the soul!

How many are sufficiently conscious that our Lord is present in the tabernacle to pay a daily visit to Him in His prison of Love? If we do not, what does it witness to but the deadening of our spiritual sense. Our body would miss a dessert more than our soul would miss a Communion.

No wonder our crucified Redeemer thirsted for us on the Cross — thirsted for our unresponsive hearts and dulled souls. And let us not think that His thirst is a proof of His need, but of our own. He does not need us for His perfection any more than we need the flower that blooms outside our window for our perfection. In dry seasons, we desire rain for the flower, not because we need the rain, but because the flower needs it.

In like manner, God thirsts for us, not because He needs us for His happiness, but because we need Him for

[66] John 4:10.

our happiness. Without Him, it is impossible for us to develop. Just as certain diseases, such as rickets and anemia, arise in the body from a deficiency of necessary vitamins, so, too, our characters fail because of a deficiency of the Spirit.

The vast majority of men and women in the world today are so underdeveloped spiritually that if a like deficiency showed in their bodies, they would be physical monstrosities.

How many millions of minds there are today that are devoid of one single satisfying truth that they can carry through life to sustain them in their sorrows and console them at their death? How many millions of wills there are that have not yet found the goal of life and that, because they are presently without it, flit like butterflies from one colored emotion to another, unable to find repose? Let them cultivate a taste for something more than bread and circuses; let them sound the depths of their beings to discover there the arid wastes crying for the refreshment of everlasting fountains.

Of course, these emaciated hungry souls are not altogether to blame. They have heard preachers without end preaching, "Go to Christ!" But what does that mean? Go back two thousand years? If so, then have they not a right to doubt the divinity of Him who could not project Himself through time?

Look up to Heaven? If so, then what has become of His blessing, His forgiveness of sinners, His Truth that He said would endure unto the end of time? Where is His authority? His power? His life now? If it is not someplace on earth, then why did He come to earth? To leave only the echo of His words, the record of His deeds, and then to slip away leaving us only a history and its teachers?

Somewhere on earth today is His truth: "He that heareth you, heareth me."[67] Somewhere on earth is His power: "Behold, I have given you power...."[68] Somewhere on earth is His life: "The bread that I will give is my flesh, for the life of the world."[69] Where to find it?

There is an institution on the face of the earth that claims to possess all these things, and to those who have knocked at its portals and have asked for a drink has come the elixir of divine life and, with it, the peace that comes to those who drink and never thirst again, and eat and never hunger again.

[67] Luke 10:16.

[68] Luke 10:19.

[69] John 6:52 (RSV = John 6:51).

To each and every one of us, inside and outside the Church, our Lord asks, "Will you accept the cup of my love?" He took our cup of hate and bitterness in Gethsemane, and its dregs were so bitter that they made Him cry out, "My Father, if it be possible, let this chalice pass from me."[70]

But He drank every drop of it. If He drank our cup of hates, why do we not drink His chalice of pardon? Why, then, when He cries, "I thirst," do we give Him vinegar and gall?

> I cannot tell the half of it, yet hear
> What rush of feeling still comes back to me,
> From that proud torture hanging on His Cross,
> From that gold rapture of His Heart in mine.
> I knew in blissful anguish what it means
> To be a part of Christ, and feel as mine
> The dark distresses of my brother limbs,
> To feel it bodily and simply true,
> To feel as mine the starving of His poor,
> To feel as mine the shadow of curse on all,
> Hard words, hard looks, and savage misery,

[70] Matt. 26:39.

Victory Over Vice

And struggling deaths, unpitied and unwept.
To feel rich brothers' sad satieties,
The weary manner of their lives and deaths,
That want in love, and lacking love lack all.
To feel the heavy sorrow of the world
Thicken and thicken on to future hell,
To mighty cities with their miles of streets,
Where men seek work for days, and walk
    and starve,
Freezing on riverbanks on winter nights,
And come at last to cord or stream or steel.

The horror of the things our brothers bear!
It was but naught to that which after came,
The woe of things we make our brothers bear,
Our brothers and our sisters! In my heart
Christ's Heart seemed beating, and the world's
    whole sin —
Its crimson malice and grey negligence.
Rose up and blackening hid the Face of God.

Arthur Shearly Cripps

The Sixth Word

ﻼ

Sloth

"It is finished."

John 19:30

Sloth is a malady of the will that causes us to neglect our duties. Sloth may be physical or spiritual. It is physical when it shows itself in laziness, procrastination, idleness, softness, indifference, and nonchalance. It is spiritual when it shows itself in an indifference to character betterment, a distaste for the spiritual, a hurried crowding of devotions, lukewarmness, and failure to cultivate virtue.

The classic description of the effects of sloth is to be found in the book of Proverbs: "I passed by the field of the slothful man, and by the vineyard of the foolish man. And behold, it was all filled with nettles, and thorns had covered the face thereof, and the stone wall was broken down. Which, when I had seen, I laid it up in my heart, and by the example I received instruction. Thou wilt sleep a little, said I, thou wilt slumber a little, thou wilt fold thy hands a little to rest; and poverty shall come to thee as a runner, and beggary as an armed man."[71]

Of such indifference to duty our Lord spoke in the book of Revelation: "But because thou art lukewarm, and neither cold, nor hot, I will begin to vomit thee out of my mouth."[72]

The life and teaching of our Lord lend no support to the slothful man. When yet only twelve years of age, He speaks of being about His "Father's business,"[73] which was nothing less than redeeming the world. Then, for eighteen years, He worked as a manual laborer, transforming dead and useless things into the child's crib, the friend's table, Nazarene roofs, and the farmers' wagons, as symbols of His later work by which He would transform hard money-changers and prostitutes into useful citizens of the kingdom of Heaven.

Beginning His public life with calloused hands, He preached the gospel of work: "I must work the works of

[71] Prov. 24:30-34.
[72] Apoc. 3:16 (RSV = Rev. 3:16).
[73] Luke 2:49.

Him that sent me, whilst it is day; the night cometh, when no man can work."[74] His whole life, in His own words, was spent not in receiving, but in giving: "The Son of Man is not come to be ministered unto, but to minister, and to give His life as a redemption for many."[75]

He earned the right to teach the necessity of work, and lest we live under any illusions that any other work is more important than the saving of souls, even the burial of our fathers, He said to the disciple who asked for such permission, "Follow me, and let the dead bury their dead."[76]

To the young man who wished to be His disciple, but first wanted to bid farewell to friends at home, our Lord said, "No man putting his hand to the plough, and looking back, is fit for the kingdom of God."[77] Laboring for bread alone is no fulfillment of His commandment, for to those who wanted more bread, He pleaded, "Labor not for the meat which perisheth, but for that which endureth unto life everlasting, which the Son of Man will give you."[78]

[74] John 9:4.
[75] Matt. 20:28.
[76] Matt. 8:22.
[77] Luke 9:62.
[78] John 6:27.

Victory Over Vice

The business of salvation is no easy task. There are two roads through this world and two gates into the future life. "Enter ye in at the narrow gate; for wide is the gate, and broad is the way, that leadeth to destruction, and many there are who go in thereat. How narrow is the gate, and strait is the way that leadeth to life; and few there are that find it!"[79]

Curiously enough, His invitation goes out only to those who labor for the eternal prize: "Come to me, all you who labor, and are burdened, and I will refresh you. Take up my yoke upon you, and learn of me, for I am meek, and humble of heart. And you shall find rest to your souls. For my yoke is sweet, and my burden light."[80]

So completely had He fulfilled the smallest detail of His Father's business that on the very night of His agony, in the Upper Room in the presence of His Apostles, He could raise His eyes to Heaven and pray, "Father, I have glorified Thee on earth; I have finished the work which Thou gavest me to do."[81] Then, the following afternoon, as the Carpenter is put to death by His own profession, He

[79] Matt. 7:13-14.
[80] Matt. 11:28-30.
[81] Cf. John 17:4.

cries out from the Cross, in a loud voice, the final reparation for sloth and the song of triumph: "It is consummated."

He did not say, "I die," because death did not come to take Him. He walked to it to conquer it. The last drop in the chalice of redemption was drained; the last nail had been driven in the mansion of the Father's House; the last brush had been touched to the canvas of salvation! His work was done!

But ours is not. It is important to realize this, for there are the slothful who justify themselves by saying they need only faith in Christ to save their souls. Surely He who worked so hard for the world's redemption came not to dispense His followers from work. The servant is not above the master.

Faith in Him alone does not save, for "faith without good works is dead."[82] It is not enough for the student to have faith in his teacher's knowledge; he must also study. It is not enough for the sick to have faith in their doctor; their organism must cooperate with him and his medicine. It is not enough to believe that Washington was the "father of our country"; we must also assume and fulfill our duties as American citizens.

[82] James 2:26.

In like manner, it is not enough to believe in Christ; we must live Christ and, to some extent, die Christ-like. His words permit of no equivocation: "And he that taketh not up his cross, and followeth me, is not worthy of me. He that findeth his life shall lose it, and he that shall lose his life for me shall find it."[83]

St. Paul understood the labor involved in being a Christian and wrote the same message to the Romans: "For if we have been planted together in the likeness of His death, we shall be also in the likeness of His Resurrection."[84] What He has done with His human nature, we must do with ours: plant it in the soil of the Cross and await the Resurrection of the eternal Easter.

Later, to the Corinthians, Paul repeated it: "As you are partakers of the sufferings, so shall you be also of the consolation."[85] And St. Peter, who knew well the scandal of the Cross, pleaded for joy in reliving the Cross: "If you partake of the sufferings of Christ, rejoice that when His glory shall be revealed, you may also be glad with exceeding joy."[86]

---

[83] Matt. 10:38-39.

[84] Rom. 6:5.

[85] 2 Cor. 1:7.

[86] 1 Pet. 4:13.

There is no hope for the spiritually slothful in these injunctions. Our Lord is the die; we must be stamped by it. He is the pattern; we must be remodeled to it. The Cross is the condition; we must be nailed to it. Our Lord loved His Cross so much that He keeps its scars even in His glory. He who had won victory over death kept the record of its wounds.

If so precious to Him, they cannot be meaningless for us. In their preservation is the reminder that we, too, must be signed with those signs and sealed with those seals.

On Judgment Day, He will say to each of us, "Show me your hands and feet. Where are your scars of victory? Have you fought no battles for truth? Have you won no wars for goodness? Have you made no enemy of evil?"

If we can prove we have been His warriors and show the scars on our apostolic hands, we shall enjoy the peace of victory. But woe unto us who come down from the Calvary of this earthly pilgrimage with hands unscarred and white!

Two lessons emerge from this Sixth Word from the Cross witnessing to Christ's finished work and our own unfinished tasks: First, we must beware of spiritual sloth, for its penalties are tremendous; and second, we must work for a complete life.

Victory Over Vice

The Gospel records three instances of sloth. There were the foolish virgins, chaste but lazy. The wise virgins fill their lamps with oil and wait to hear the step of the approaching bridegroom. The foolish virgins do not think of oil, and tired of waiting, they fall asleep. When the bridegroom comes, the wise virgins light their lamps and welcome the bridegroom. The foolish virgins go out to buy oil, but everybody is asleep; the shops are closed. They go back to the wedding feast, but the door is closed. They cry, "Lord, Lord, open to us." But His answer is: "Amen, I say to you, I know you not." Our Lord concludes the parable with these words: "Watch, ye, therefore, because you know not the day nor the hour."[87]

The second instance of sloth was the parable of the barren fig tree: "And the next day, when they came out from Bethania, He was hungry. And when He had seen afar off a fig tree having leaves, He came if perhaps He might find anything on it. And when He was come to it, He found nothing but leaves. For it was not the time for figs. And answering, He said to it, 'May no man hereafter eat fruit of thee anymore forever.' "[88]

[87] Matt. 25:1-13.
[88] Mark 11:12-14.

The third was the parable of the buried talent. He who received five talents earned another five; he who had received two earned another two; but he who received one hid it in the ground. Of him the lord of the servants said, "Wicked and slothful servant! . . . Take ye away, therefore, the talent from him, and give it him that hath ten talents. For to everyone that hath shall be given, and he shall abound: but from him that hath not, that also which he seemeth to have shall be taken away. And the unprofitable servant cast ye out into the exterior darkness. There shall be weeping and gnashing of teeth."[89]

Common to these three parables is the danger of sloth and the necessity of work. Purity without good works will not save us any more than it saved the foolish virgins. Those who do nothing run the risk of losing the little they have. In other words, it is possible to lose our souls by doing nothing. "How shall we escape if we neglect . . . ?" We lose our souls not only by the evil we do, but also by the good we leave undone.

Neglect the body, and the muscles stiffen; neglect the mind, and imbecility comes; neglect the soul, and ruin follows. Just as physical life is the sum of the forces that

[89] Matt. 25:26, 28-30.

resist death, so the spiritual life is to some extent the sum of the forces that resist evil. Neglect to take an antidote for a poison in the body, and we die by our neglect. Neglect to take precaution against sin, and we die the death merely because of neglect.

Heaven is a city on a hill. Hence, we cannot coast into it; we have to climb. Those who are too lazy to mount can miss its capture as well as the evil who refuse to seek it. Let no one think he can be totally indifferent to God in this life and suddenly develop a capacity for Him at the moment of death.

Where will the capacity for Heaven come from if we have neglected it on earth? A man cannot suddenly walk into a lecture room on higher mathematics and be thrilled by its equations if all during life he neglected to develop a taste for mathematics. A heaven of poets would be a hell to those who never learned to love poetry. And a heaven of divine truth, righteousness, and justice would be a hell to those who never studiously cultivated those virtues here below. Heaven is only for those who work for Heaven.

If we crush every inspiration of the Divine; if we drown every Godward inspiration of the soul; if we choke every inlet to Christ — where will be our relish for God on the last day? The very things we neglected will then be the very cause of our ruin. The very things that should have ministered to our growth will then turn against us and minister to our decay.

The sun that warms the plant can, under other conditions, also wither it. The rain that nourishes the flower can, under other conditions, rot it. The same sun shines upon mud that shines upon wax. It hardens the mud but softens the wax. The difference is not in the sun, but in that upon which it shines.

So it is with God. The divine life that shines upon a soul who loves Him, softens it into everlasting life; that same divine life that shines upon the slothful soul, neglectful of God, hardens it into everlasting death.

Heaven and Hell are, in like manner, both effects of divine goodness. Their difference comes from our reaction to that goodness and, to that extent, are also our creations. Both God and man are in different senses creators of Heaven and Hell.

A little heed, then, to this word from the Cross: "It is consummated." We finish our vocation as He finished His — on a cross and nowhere else. Only to the doers of the truth, and not to its preachers or its hearers, comes the reward of the crown. Doing implies the spending not of what we *have*, but of what we *are*.

Victory Over Vice

We need have no undue fear for our health if we work hard for the kingdom of God. God will take care of our health if we take care of His cause. In any case, it is better to burn out than to rust out.

Burning the candle at both ends for God's sake may be foolishness to the world, but it is a profitable Christian exercise — for so much better the light. Only one thing in life matters: being found worthy of the Light of the World in the hour of His visitation.

"Take ye heed," He said. "Take ye heed, watch and pray. For ye know not when the time is. Even as a man who going into a far country, left his house, and gave authority to his servants over every work, and commanded the porter to watch. Watch ye therefore (for you know not when the lord of the house cometh: at even, or at midnight, or at the cock crowing, or in the morning), lest coming on a sudden, he find you sleeping. And what I say to you, I say to all: Watch."[90]

Not only must we beware of spiritual sloth, but we must also work for a completed life. The important word in the struggle against sloth is *finished*. The world judges us by results; our Lord judges us by the way we fulfill and

[90] Mark 13:33-37.

finish our appointed tasks. A good life is not necessarily a successful life.

The sowers are not always the reapers. Those whom God destines only to sow receive their reward for just that, even though they never garnered a single sheaf into everlasting barns. In the parable of the talents, the reward is according to the development of potentialities and the completion of appointed duties.

One day, our Lord, "sitting over against the treasury, beheld how the people cast money into the treasury, and many that were rich cast in much. And there came a certain poor widow, and she cast in two mites, which make about half a cent. And calling His disciples together, He saith to them, 'Amen, I say to you, this poor widow hath cast in more than all they who have cast into the treasury. For all they did cast in of their abundance; but she of her want cast in all she had, even her whole living.' "[91]

The result was trivial for the treasury, but it was infinite for her soul. She had not half-done her duty; she had finished it. This is what is meant by completed living.

In the Christian order, it is not the important who are essential, nor those who do great things who are really

[91] Mark 12:41-44.

great. A king is no nobler in the sight of God than a peasant. The head of government, with millions of troops at his command, is no more precious in the sight of God than a paralyzed child. The former has greater opportunities for evil, but like the widow in the Temple, if the child fulfills his task of resignation to the will of God more than the dictator fulfills his task of procuring social justice for the glory of God, then the child is greater. "God is no respecter of persons."[92]

Men and women are only actors on the stage of life. Why should he who plays the part of the rich man glory in his gold and rich table and consider himself better than one who plays the role of the beggar begging a crumb from his table. When the curtain goes down, they are both men.

So when God pulls down the curtain on the drama of the world's redemption, He will not ask what part we played, but only how well we played the role assigned to us. The Little Flower[93] has said that one could save one's soul by picking up pins out of love of God.

[92] Cf. Acts 10:34.

[93] St. Thérèse of Lisieux (1873-1897), Carmelite nun and Doctor.

Sloth

If we could create worlds and drop them into space from our fingertips, we would please God no more than by dropping a coin into a tin cup. It is not what is done, but *why* it is done that matters. A bootblack shining a pair of shoes inspired by a divine motive is doing more good for this world than all the godless conventions Moscow could ever convene.

It is the intention that makes the work. Duties in life are like marble, canvas, and stone. Marble becomes valuable because of the image given to it by the sculptor; canvas is ennobled by the picture of the artist; and stone is glorified by the pattern of the architect.

So it is with our works. The intention gives them value as the image gives the marble value. God is not interested in what we do with our hands, or our money, or our minds, or our mouths, but with our wills. It is not the work but the worker that counts.

Let those souls who think their work has no value recognize that, by fulfilling their insignificant tasks out of a love of God, those tasks assume a supernatural worth. The aged who bear the taunts of the young, the sick crucified to their beds, the ignorant immigrant in the steel mill, the street cleaner and the garbage collector, the wardrobe mistress in the theater and the chorus girl who never had

a line, the unemployed carpenter and the ash collector —
all these will be enthroned above dictators, presidents,
kings, and cardinals if a greater love of God inspires their
humbler tasks than inspires those who play nobler roles
with less love.

No work is finished until we do it for the honor and
glory of God. "Whether you eat or drink, or whatever else
you do, do all to the glory of God."[94] When our lease on
life runs out, two questions will be asked. The world will
ask, "How much did he leave?" The angels will ask, "How
much did he bring with him?"

The soul can carry much, but in its journey to the judgment seat of God, it will be freighted down only with that
kind of goods which a man can carry away from a ship-
wreck — his good works done for the glory of God. All
that we leave behind is "unfinished." All that we take
with us is "finished."

May we never die too soon! This does not mean not
dying young; it means not dying with our appointed tasks
undone. It is indeed a curious fact that no one ever thinks
of our Lord as dying too young! That is because He finished His Father's business. But no matter how old we are

[94] 1 Cor. 10:31.

when we die, we always feel there is something more to be done.

Why do we feel that way, if it is not because we did not do well the tasks assigned to us? Our task may not be great; it may be only to add one stone to the Temple of God. But whatever it is, do each tiny little act in union with your Savior, who died on the Cross, and you will finish your life. Then you will never die too young!

> But if, impatient, thou let slip thy cross,
> Thou wilt not find it in this world again,
> Nor in another; here, and here alone
> Is given thee to suffer for God's sake.
> In other worlds we shall more perfectly
> Serve Him and love Him, praise Him, work
>   for Him,
> Grow near and nearer Him with all delight;
>
> But then we shall not anymore be called
> To suffer, which is our appointment here.
> Canst thou not suffer then one hour — or two?
> If He should call thee from thy cross today,
>
> Saying, "It is finished!" — that hard cross of thine,
> From which thou prayest for deliverance,

Victory Over Vice

Thinkest thou not some passion of regret
Would overcome thee? Thou wouldst say, "So
    soon?
Let me go back and suffer yet awhile

More patiently. I have not yet praised God."
And He might answer to thee, "Nevermore.
All pain is done with." Whensoe'er it comes,
That summons that we look for, it will seem
Soon, yea too soon. Let us take heed in time
That God may now be glorified in us;
And while we suffer, let us set our souls
To suffer perfectly: since this alone,
The suffering, which is this world's special grace
May here be perfected and left behind. . . .
Endure, endure — be faithful to the end!

Harriet Eleanor Hamilton-King

The Seventh Word

࿔

Covetousness

"Father, into Thy hands,
I commend my spirit."

Luke 23:46

Covetousness is an inordinate love of the things of this world. It becomes inordinate if one is not guided by a reasonable end, such as a suitable provision for one's family, or the future, or if one is too solicitous in amassing wealth, or too parsimonious in dispensing it. The sin of covetousness includes, therefore, both the intention one has in acquiring the goods of this world and the manner of acquiring them. It is not the love of an excessive sum that makes it wrong, but an inordinate love of any sum.

Simply because a man has a great fortune, it does not follow that he is a covetous man. A child with a few pennies might possibly be more covetous. Material things are lawful and necessary to enable us to live according to our station in life, to mitigate suffering, to advance the kingdom of God, and to save our souls.

It is the pursuit of wealth as an end, instead of a means to the above ends, that makes a man covetous.

In this class of the covetous are to be placed the young woman who marries a divorced man for his money; the public official who accepts a bribe; the capitalist who puts profits above human rights and needs, and the laborer who puts party power above the laborer's rights.

Covetousness is much more general in the world today than we suspect. It once was monopolized by the avaricious rich; now it is shared by the envious poor. Because a man has no money in his pockets is no proof that he is not covetous; he may be involuntarily poor with a passion for wealth far in excess of those who possess.

History bears witness to the fact that almost every radical economic revolutionist in history has been interested in only one thing: booty. The only poor people who ever attacked the rich and sought nothing for themselves were our Lord and His followers, like St. Francis of Assisi.[95]

---

[95] St. Francis of Assisi (1182-1226), founder of the Franciscan Order.

There are very few disinterested lovers of the poor today; most of their so-called champions do not love the poor as much as they hate the rich. They hate all the rich, but they love only those poor who will help them attain their wicked ends.

Such covetousness is ruinous for man, principally because it hardens the heart. Man becomes like unto that which he loves, and if he loves gold, he becomes like it — cold, hard, and yellow. The more he acquires, the more he suffers at surrendering even the least of it, just as it hurts to have a single hair pulled out even though your head is full of them.

The more the sinfully rich man gets, the more he believes he is needy. He is always poor in his own eyes. The sense of the spiritual thus becomes so deadened that its most precious treasures are bartered away for the trivial increases, as Judas sold his Master for thirty pieces of silver.

As St. Paul tells us, "The desire for money is the root of all evils, which some coveting have erred from the Faith."[96] The Providence of God becomes less and less a reality, and if it still retains value, it is reduced to a secondary role; God is trusted as long as we have a good bank account.

[96] 1 Tim. 6:10.

Victory Over Vice

When things go well, we are quite willing to dispense with God, like the young man in the Gospel who came to our Lord only because he was being deprived of some of his father's estate. "Master, speak to my brother that he divide the inheritance with me."[97] It was only when economic confusion arose that the young man had recourse to the Divine.

There are many in the world today who think that the only reason for the existence of the Church is to improve the economic order, and if they do not have their fill, they assail the Church for failing. Well indeed might the Church answer in the words of our Lord: "O man, who hath appointed me judge and divider over you?"[98]

To turn man's heart away from perishable things to the eternal values of the soul was one of the reasons for the Lord's visit to the earth. His teaching from the beginning was not only a warning against covetousness, but a plea for a greater trust in Providence.

"Do not lay up for yourselves treasures upon the earth, where moth and rust consume, and where thieves break through and steal; but lay up for yourselves treasures in

[97] Luke 12:13.
[98] Luke 12:14.

Heaven, where neither moth nor rust consumes, and where thieves do not break through nor steal. For where thy treasure is, there will thy heart be also."[99]

> I say to you therefore, do not be anxious about your life, what you shall eat or what you shall drink; nor about your body, what you shall wear. Is not the life of more consequence than the food, and the body than the clothing? Look at the birds of the sky, how they neither sow nor reap nor gather into barns, yet your heavenly Father feeds them! Are you not of much more value than they? Yet who among you by anxious thought is able to add a single span to his life?
>
> And why should you worry about clothing? Observe the field-lilies, how they grow; they neither toil nor spin; yet I tell you that even Solomon in all his magnificence was not arrayed like one of them. But if God so clothes the grass of the field, which exists today and is thrown in the oven tomorrow, will He not much rather clothe you, O you of little faith?

[99] Matt. 6:19-21.

Do not therefore worry saying, "What shall we eat?" "What shall we drink?" or "What shall we wear?" for the heathen seek after all these things; and your heavenly Father knows that you need them all. But seek first the kingdom of God and His holiness, and all these things shall be given you besides. Do not then be anxious about tomorrow, for tomorrow will take care of itself. Quite enough for the day is its own trouble.[100]

The man who unduly loves riches is a fallen man, because of a bad exchange; he might have had Heaven through his generosity, and he has only the earth. He could have kept his soul, but he sold it for material things. Camels will pass through eyes of needles more easily than the covetous will pass through the gates of Heaven. It was easy, of course, to condemn the rich; our world is too full of those who are doing it now. But our economic revolutionists do it because they envy wealth, not because they love poverty.

It was not so with our divine Savior. He who condemned Dives and the man who ordered bigger barns the

[100]Matt. 6:25-34.

very day he died, and who thundered that no man could serve God and mammon, lived His gospel. Not in a hospital, or a home, or a city, but in a stable in the fields did He bow entrance into the world He made. Not with money did He make money in the markets of exchange, but as a poor carpenter.

He earned His living with the two most primitive instruments used: wood and hammer. During His three years of preaching, not even a roof could He claim as His own: "The foxes have burrows, and the birds of the sky have nests; but the Son of Man has not a place where He may lay His head."

Then, at His death, He had no wealth to leave; His Mother he gave to John; His body to the tomb; His blood to the earth; His garments to His executioners. Absolutely dispossessed, He is still hated, to give the lie to those who say religion is hated because of its possessions.

Religion is hated because it is religion, and possessions are only the excuse and pretext for driving God from the earth. There was no quarreling about His will; there was no dispute about how His property would be divided; there was no lawsuit over the Lord of the universe.

He had given up everything in reparation for covetousness, keeping only one thing for Himself that was not a thing: His Spirit. With a loud cry, so powerful that it freed His soul from His flesh and bore witness to the fact that He was giving up His life and not having it taken away, He said in farewell, "Father, into Thy hands I commend my spirit."

It rang out over the darkness and lost itself in the furthermost ends of the earth. The world has made all kinds of noise since to drown it out.

Men have busied themselves with nothing to shut out hearing it; but through the fog and darkness of cities, and the silence of the night, that awful cry rings within the hearing of everyone who does not force himself to forget, and as we listen to it, we learn two lessons: the more ties we have to earth, the harder will it be for us to die; and we were never meant to be perfectly satisfied here below.

In every friendship, hearts grow and entwine themselves together, so that the two hearts seem to make only one heart with only a common thought. That is why separation is so painful. It is not so much two hearts separating, but one heart being torn asunder.

When a man loves wealth inordinately, he and it grow together like a tree pushing itself in growth through the crevices of a rock. Death to such a man is a painful wrench, because of his close identification with the material. He has everything to live for, nothing to die for. He becomes at death the most destitute and despoiled beggar in the universe, for he has nothing he can take with him. He discovers too late that he did not belong to himself, but to things, for wealth is a pitiless master.

It would not allow him during life to think of anything else except increasing itself. Now he discovers too late that by consecrating himself to filling his barns, he was never free to save the only thing he could carry with him to eternity: his soul. In order to acquire a part, he lost the whole. He won a fraction of the earth; now he will need only six feet of it.

Like a giant tied down by ten thousand ropes to ten thousand stakes, he is no longer free to think about anything else than what he must leave. That is why death is so hard for the covetous rich.

On the contrary, as the ties to earth become lessened, the easier is the separation. Where our treasure is, there is our heart also. If we have lived for God, then death is a liberation. Earth and its possessions are the cage that confines us, and death is the opening of its door, enabling our soul to wing its way to its Beloved, for which it had only lived and for which it only waited to die.

Victory Over Vice

Our powers of dispossession are greater than our powers of possession; our hands could never contain all the gold in the world, but we can wash our hands of its desire. We cannot own the world, but we can disown it. That is why the soul with the vow of poverty is more satisfied than the richest covetous man in the world, for the latter has not yet all he wants, while the religious wants nothing; in a certain sense, the religious has all and is perfectly happy.

It was such poverty of spirit raised to its most sublime peak that made the death of our Lord so easy. He had no ties to earth. His treasure was with the Father, and His soul followed the spiritual law of gravitation.

Cold, like dirt, falls; charity, like fire, rises: "Father, into Thy hands I commend my spirit."

The death of our Lord on the Cross reveals that we are meant to be perpetually dissatisfied here below. If earth were meant to be a Paradise, then He who made it would never have taken leave of it on Good Friday. The commending of the spirit to the Father was at the same time the refusal to commend it to earth. The completion or fulfillment of life is in Heaven, not on earth.

Our Lord in His last word is saying that nowhere else can we be satisfied except in God. It is absolutely impossible for us to be perfectly happy here below. Nothing proves this more than disappointment. One might almost say the essence of life is disappointment.

We look forward to a position, to marriage, to ownership, to power, to popularity, to wealth, and when we attain them, we have to admit, if we are honest, that they never come up to our expectations.

As children, we looked forward to Christmas; when it came and we had our fill of sweets and tested every toy or rocked every doll, and then crept into our beds, we said in our own little heart of hearts: "Somehow or other, it did not quite come up to expectations." That experience is repeated a thousand times in life.

But why is there disappointment? Because when we look forward to a future ideal, we endow it with something of the infinity of the soul. I can imagine a house with ten thousand rooms studded with diamonds and emeralds, but I shall never see one. I can imagine a mountain of gold, but I shall never see one.

So with our earthly ideals. We color them with the qualities of our spiritual soul. But when they become realized, they are concrete, cabined, cribbed, confined. A tremendous disproportion thus arises between the ideal we conceived and the reality before us.

Victory Over Vice

That disproportion between the infinite and the finite is the cause of disappointment. There is no escaping this fact. We have eternity in our heart, but time on our hands. The soul demands a heaven, and we get only an earth. Our eyes look up to the mountains, but they rest only on the plains. It is easier to strangle our ideals than it is to satisfy them. He who attains his earthly ideal smashes it.

To touch an ideal in this world is to destroy the ideal. "No man is a hero to his valet." We are no longer thirsty at the border of a well. The satisfaction of earthly ideals turns against us, like a cruel retort from one we paid an underhand compliment.

But there is no reason for being pessimists or cynics. Disappointment is no proof that there is no ideal, but only that it is not here. Just as we would have no eyes were there no beauties to see, and as we would have no ears were there no harmonies to hear, so we would have no appetite for the infinite were there no God to love.

In Him alone is the reconciliation of the chase and the capture. Here on this earth, we are buffeted between the two. The chase has its thrill, for it is the pursuit of an ideal, the quest for satisfaction, and the march to victory. The capture, too, has its thrill, for it is possession, enjoyment, and peace.

But while we live in time, we can never enjoy both together. The capture ends the excitement of the chase; and the chase without a capture is maddening, like having a refreshing spring withdrawn from our parched lips as we draw near to it.

How to combine the chase without the ennui of capture, and the capture without losing the joy of the chase?

It is impossible here below, but not in Heaven, for when we attain unto God, we capture the infinite, and because He is infinite, it will take an eternity of chase to discover the undiscoverable joys of life, truth, love, and beauty.

Such is the meaning behind the last and farewell word from the Cross. Centuries ago the sun shone upon plants and trees and imprisoned within them its light and heat. Today we dig up that light and heat in coal, and as its flames mount upward, we pay back our debt to the sun.

So now the divine Light, which for thirty-three years has been imprisoning Itself in human hearts, goes back again to the Father, ever to remind us that only by completing a similar circuit and commending our souls to the Father do we find the answer to the riddle of life, and the end of disappointment and the beginning of eternal peace for our eternal hearts.

Victory Over Vice

Everything is disappointing except the redemptive love of our Lord. You can go on acquiring things, but you will be poor until your soul is filled with the love of Him who died on the Cross for you. As the eye was made for seeing and the ear for hearing, so your spirit was made to be recommended back again to God.

If it had any other destiny, the dying words of the Savior would have betrayed that destiny. The spirit has a capacity for the infinite; the knowledge of one flower, the life of a single hour, the love of a minute do not exhaust its potencies. It wants the fullness of these things; in a word, it wants God.

The tragedy of our modern life is that so many put their pleasures in desires rather than in discovery. Having lost the one purpose of human living — namely, God — they seek substitutes in the petty things of earth.

After repeated disappointments, they begin to put their happiness not in a pleasure, but in the hunt for it, in butterfly existences that never rest long enough at any one moment to know their inner desires; running races, hoping they will never end; turning pages but never discovering the plot; knocking at doors of truth and then dashing away, lest its portals be opened and they be invited in. Existence becomes a flight from peace, rather than an advance; a momentary escape from frustration instead of its sublimation in victory.

Every now and then, there comes to some a light through the clouds of Calvary and the echo of the word commending a spirit to God, but instead of making a supreme effort to satisfy the goal of life, they crucify it.

"But the husbandmen said one to another, 'This is the heir; come, let us kill him and the inheritance shall be ours.' And laying hold of him, they killed him and cast him out of the vineyard."[101]

Thus do some men believe that if they could drive God from the earth, the inheritance of sin would be there without remorse; and if they could but silence conscience, they could inherit peace without justice. It was just this mentality that sent our Lord to the Cross. If the voice of God could be stifled, they believed they could enjoy the voice of Satan in peace.

Now take a different outlook on the world. How many, even of those who have killed conscience, can say, "I am happy; there is nothing I want"? But if you are not brave enough to say that, then why not seek? And why not seek in the one direction in which you know happiness lies?

[101]Mark 12:7-8.

Victory Over Vice

At death, you will leave everything, but there is one thing you will not leave: your desire for life. You want the one thing the Cross brings you: life through death.

In its effulgence, the mystery of existence becomes clear. The Cross refers to me, personally and individually as if no one else in the world ever existed. On the Cross, Christ has traced for me in sacrifice, which is the most sublime of gestures, a program of life, submission to the divine will. He went down the dark road of Gethsemane to Calvary's death out of devotedness to God's glory and my salvation.

For my culpable self-indulgence, He atones by surrender of Himself. "He was wounded for our iniquities; He was bruised for our sins. The chastisement of our peace was upon Him."[102]

If this Master of the world's symphony would miss my single note of virtue in the harmony of the universe; if this Captain of wars would miss my spear in His battle for goodness; if this Artist would miss my little daub of color in the masterpiece of redemption; if this cosmic Architect would note the absence of my little stone in the building of His temple; if this Tree of Life would feel the fall of but

[102]Isa. 53: 5.

my little leaf to the sinfulness of earth; if this heavenly Father would miss me in the empty chair at the banquet spread for the millions of the children of God; if this Orator from the pulpit of the Cross would note my inattention as I turned to glance at an executioner; if God cares that much for me, then I must be worth something, since He loves me so!

But if Himself He come to thee, and stand
Beside thee, gazing down on thee with eyes
That smile, and suffer; that will smite thy
   heart,
With their own pity, to a passionate peace;
And reach to thee Himself and the Holy Cup
(With all its wreathen stems of passion-flowers
And quivering sparkles of the ruby stars),
Pallid and royal, saying, "Drink with me";
Wilt thou refuse? Nay, not for Paradise!
The pale brow will compel thee, the pure
   hands
Will minister unto thee; thou shalt take
Of that communion through the solemn depths
Of the dark waters of thine agony,
With heart that praises Him, that yearns to Him

Victory Over Vice

The closer through that hour. Hold fast His hand
Though the nails pierce thine too! Take only care
Lest one drop of the sacramental wine
Be spilled, of that which ever shall unite
Thee, soul and body, to thy living Lord!

Harriet Eleanor Hamilton-King

Fulton J. Sheen

(1895-1979)

Pope John Paul II once said to Fulton Sheen, "You have written and spoken well of the Lord Jesus." But the popular priest whom millions watched weekly on television had a humbler view of himself: "The Lord once used an ass to ride to Jerusalem. Now He uses an ass on TV." In his witty way, he recognized himself as an instrument of Christ.

Fulton John Sheen was born in El Paso, Illinois. In high school, he won a university scholarship, but turned it down to pursue a vocation to the priesthood. He attended St. Viator College and Seminary in Bourbannais, Illinois, and St. Paul Seminary in St. Paul, Minnesota. In 1919, he was ordained a priest for the Diocese of Peoria. He then earned graduate degrees at the Catholic University of America and at Catholic University of Louvain, Belgium.

Victory Over Vice

In his studies, Sheen sought to learn two things: "First, what the modern world is thinking about; second, how to answer the errors of modern philosophy in the light of the philosophy of St. Thomas." Indeed, St. Thomas Aquinas influenced him greatly. Sheen's goal was to "make St. Thomas functional, not for a school, but for a world . . . a remedy against the anarchy of ideas, riot of philosophical systems, and breakdown of spiritual forces."

Sheen received numerous teaching offers, but turned them down in obedience to his bishop and became an assistant pastor in a rural parish. His bishop later permitted him to teach at Catholic University of America and at St. Edmund's College, Ware, England, where he met G. K. Chesterton, whose BBC radio broadcast inspired Sheen's later NBC broadcast "The Catholic Hour" (1930-1952).

In 1952, Sheen began appearing on ABC in his own series, "Life Is Worth Living." Despite being given a time slot that forced him to compete with Milton Berle and Frank Sinatra, the dynamic Sheen enjoyed enormous success and in 1954 reached twenty-five million viewers — non-Catholics as well as Catholics. He designed his presentations for viewers of all faiths and backgrounds and covered a wide range of topics, which he approached from the perspective of Christian humanism.

Fulton J. Sheen

His weekly television program made Sheen one of the country's most well-known priests. But even off the screen he was winning souls for Christ. His courses attracted people from diverse backgrounds, and his powerful, eloquent preaching won many to the Faith.

He gave annual Good Friday homilies at New York's St. Patrick's Cathedral, gave numerous retreats for priests and religious, and preached at summer conferences in Cambridge, England and London's Westminster Cathedral. In 1948, he accompanied Cardinal Spellman on a forty-day Pacific Tour, during which he preached more than two hundred times.

Sheen served as Bishop of Rochester, New York (1966-1969) and Auxiliary Bishop of New York (1951-1966). While he was National Director of the Society for the Propagation of the Faith (SPF), the Church's overseas mission, to which he donated what he was paid for his television appearances, donations to the SPF soared. Sheen traveled to missions in other countries and founded and edited *Mission* magazine to reveal the plight of the poor throughout the world. He served on the Commission on the Missions at Vatican II and in 1969 was appointed by Pope Paul VI to the Papal Commission for Nonbelievers and named Titular Archbishop of Newport, Wales.

"If you want people to stay as they are," Sheen said, "tell them what they want to hear. If you want to improve them, tell them what they should know." This he did, not only in his preaching, but also in the more than ninety books he wrote. His *Peace of Soul* was sixth on the *New York Times'* bestseller list.

Sheen's two great loves were for the Blessed Mother and for the Eucharist. He made a daily holy hour in front of the Blessed Sacrament, from which he drew strength and inspiration to preach the gospel and in the presence of which he prepared his homilies. "I beg [Christ] every day to keep me strong physically and alert mentally in order to preach His gospel and proclaim His Cross and Resurrection," he said. "I am so happy doing this that I sometimes feel that when I come to the good Lord in Heaven, I will take a few days' rest and then ask Him to allow me to come back again to this earth to do some more work."

The good Lord called Fulton J. Sheen home in 1979. His television broadcasts, now on tape, and his books continue his earthly work of winning souls for Christ. Sheen's cause for canonization has been opened in Rome.

An Invitation

Reader, the book that you hold in your hands was published by Sophia Institute Press.

Sophia Institute seeks to restore man's knowledge of eternal truth, including man's knowledge of his own nature, his relation to other persons, and his relation to God.

Our press fulfills this mission by offering translations, reprints, and new publications. We offer scholarly as well as popular publications; there are works of fiction along with books that draw from all the arts and sciences of our civilization. These books afford readers a rich source of the enduring wisdom of mankind.

Sophia Institute Press is the publishing arm of the Thomas More College of Liberal Arts and Holy Spirit College. Both colleges are dedicated to providing university-level education in the Western tradition under the guiding light of Catholic teaching.

If you know a young person who might be interested in the ideas found in this book, share it. If you know a young person seeking a college that takes seriously the adventure of learning and the quest for truth, bring our institutions to his attention.

www.SophiaInstitute.com
www.ThomasMoreCollege.edu
www.HolySpiritCollege.org

SOPHIA INSTITUTE PRESS

THE PUBLISHING DIVISION OF